# TOP
# NORMANDY

FIONA DUNCAN AND
LEONIE GLASS

# Top 10 Normandy Highlights

# The Top 10 of Everything

# CONTENTS

## Normandy Area by Area

## Streetsmart

Within each Top 10 list in this book, no hierarchy of quality or popularity is implied. All 10 are, in the editor's opinion, of roughly equal merit.

**Front cover and spine** *Château Gaillard, a 12th-century fortress built by Richard the Lionheart above Les Andelys*
**Back cover** *The port of Honfleur*
**Title page** *Le Vieux Bassin, Honfleur*

LA MAISON MUSEE DU FILET

# Welcome to
# Normandy

Magnificent Gothic architecture, rugged coastlines, sublime châteaux, ancient sea ports, bucolic countryside, pungent cheeses and heady ciders. These are just a few of the attractions of Normandy, a region that has inspired countless artists and writers. With Eyewitness Top 10 Normandy, it's yours to explore.

Normandy's rich and fascinating history is most apparent in the stunning island monastery of **Mont-St-Michel**, the Gothic masterpiece of **Rouen cathedral** and the tale of the Norman conquest of England depicted in the exquisite **Bayeux Tapestry**. No less absorbing are the more recent traces of history seen in the **D-Day beaches**, with their poignant memorials and cemeteries. Normandy is also full of natural splendours. Its varied coast ranges from the spectacular cliff formations at **Étretat** to the vast beaches and remote headlands of the **Cotentin**. Inland, in the **Pays d'Auge**, you will find lush, rolling countryside full of orchards, cow-grazed meadows and handsome half-timbered manor houses.

A visit to Normandy also offers the chance to indulge in some fabulous seafood and fine cuisine, not to mention cheeses and cider. To work some of it off, you can cycle along idyllic tracks, walk through ancient forests, climb the wooded peaks of the **Suisse Normande** or ride a horse through the lovely **Perche** countryside.

Whether you're coming for a weekend or a week, our Top 10 Guide brings together the best the region has to offer, from charming, rustic villages to elegant *belle époque* resorts. It provides useful tips throughout, from seeking out what's free to avoiding the worst of the crowds, plus well-designed itineraries covering the key sights. Add inspiring photography and detailed maps to the mix, and you have the essential pocket-sized travel companion. **Enjoy the book, and enjoy Normandy**.

Clockwise from top: Boats on the beach at Étretat; Pont de Normandie; Musee du Filet, La Perrière; Château Gaillard; Le Vieux Bassin, Honfleur; gargoyle at Notre-Dame, Louviers; interior of Basilique de Ste-Thérèse, Lisieux

# Exploring Normandy

Normandy boasts a scenic coastline, beautiful countryside and historic towns. To help make the most of your stay in this fascinating region, here are some ideas for two or seven days of sightseeing.

**Dramatic cliff formations** characterize the coastline at the resort of Étretat.

## Two Days in Normandy

### Day ❶

**MORNING**
Start in **Étretat** *(see pp30–31)*, one of Normandy's most appealing seaside resorts, with its dramatic coastal formations, clifftop walks and enticing seafood restaurants.

**AFTERNOON**
Head to **Honfleur** *(see pp20–21)* and explore the picturesque harbour, lined with cafés and medieval houses. Don't miss the extraordinary wooden Église Ste-Catherine, the quirky Maisons Satie and Boudin's beautiful seascape pastels at the Musée Eugène Boudin.

### Day ❷

**MORNING**
Immerse yourself in the **Pays d'Auge** *(see pp38–9)*, with its meadows, orchards and half-timbered houses. Stop off at the pretty village of **Beuvron-en-Auge** *(see p56)*, one of France's "plus beaux villages".

**AFTERNOON**
Head northeast to **Rouen** *(see pp24–7)* and admire its stunning Gothic

Cathédrale Notre-Dame and artfully restored medieval streets. There are some fine museums, notably the **Musée des Beaux-Arts** *(see p55)* and the **Historial Jeanne d'Arc** *(see p26)*, which brilliantly tells the story of Joan of Arc.

## Seven Days in Normandy

### Day ❶
Follow Day 1 of the two-day itinerary.

### Day ❷
Spend a relaxing morning in one of the seaside resorts on the **Côte Fleurie** *(see pp32–3)*, perhaps Deauville or Trouville. After lunch, visit Cabourg, associated with Marcel Proust, and go fossil-hunting along the Falaises des Vaches Noires.

### Day ❸
Tour the **D-Day beaches** *(see pp34–7)*. The broad Omaha Beach is particularly impressive; nearby are

**Key**
— Two-day itinerary
— Seven-day itinerary

**Beuvron-en-Auge** is one of the prettiest of the region's villages.

*Étretat*

SEINE-MARITIME

*Trouville*
*Deauville*
*Falaises des Vaches Noires*
*Honfleur*
*Cabourg*
*Abbey de Jumièges*
*Rouen*

*Beuvron-en-Auge*
*Pays d'Auge*
EURE
*Giverny*

*Route du Cidre*
CALVADOS

*Roche d'Oëtre*
Suisse Normande

*Sées*
ORNE
*Le Perche*
*Bellême*

**The Bayeux Tapestry** records the Norman Conquest through 58 scenes.

two museums and the American cemetery. In the afternoon, drive inland to **Bayeux** (see pp16–19) to see its famous tapestry, as well as its lovely cathedral.

## Day 4

Start out early and head south to **Granville** (see p105). Spend some time taking in the town's superb beaches and striking walled citadel. Afterwards, continue south to **Mont-St-Michel** (see pp12–15), Normandy's most spectacular sight. Cross the footbridge and explore the abbey and the rest of the island.

## Day 5

Drive inland to **La Suisse Normande** (see p95), a beguiling region of wooded hills and rocky crags. Climb up the Roche d'Oëtre for superb views of the Rouvre gorges. Pause for a spot of lunch, then continue east into the lush countryside of the **Pays d'Auge** (see pp38–9), where Normandy's famous cheeses are made. Follow the Route du Cidre and end your day with a tour of a distillery.

## Day 6

Explore Le **Perche** (see p112), an unspoiled region of undulating hills and woods, and stop off at one of its charming villages – perhaps **Sées** or **Bellême** (see p114). Afterwards, immerse yourself in Claude Monet's exquisitely beautiful garden at **Giverny** (see pp40–43).

## Day 7

Head northwest to the provincial capital of **Rouen** (see p24–7) for a morning of sightseeing and shopping. Spend the afternoon wandering among the beautiful remains of the **Abbaye de Jumièges** (see pp22–3).

# Top 10 Normandy Highlights

The Porte d'Aval and the Aiguille d'Étretat

# 🔟 Normandy Highlights

Normandy brings a variety of images to mind: William the Conqueror, the D-Day landings, Mont-St-Michel, dramatic cliffs, summer beaches, sumptuous châteaux, historic abbeys, forested peaks, fruit orchards, Monet's garden. Whatever your list, it will barely scratch the surface of this rewarding region.

## Mont-St-Michel ①

This solitary rock, dominated by a monumental abbey, became a place of pilgrimage over 1,000 years ago *(see pp12–15)*.

## ② Bayeux Tapestry

This unique historical document and work of art tells the story of the Norman Conquest of England in 1066 *(see pp16–17)*.

## ④ Abbaye de Jumièges

These magnificent, ruins – a blend of Romanesque and Gothic architecture – are all that remains of a 7th-century Benedictine abbey *(see pp22–3)*.

## Honfleur ③

A magnet for artists since the 19th century, this picturesque maritime town was also an important trade centre *(see pp20–21)*.

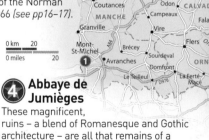

Port Racine
Cherbourg
Vauvillé
Les Pieux
Barneville-Plage
Valognes
Carentan
Lessay
Marigny
St-Lô
Coutances
MANCHE
Granville
Mont-St-Michel ①
Brécey
Avranches
Le Teilleul
Aunay-sur-Odon
Campeaux
Vire
Sourdeval
Domfront
D-Day Beaches ⑧
Baie de la Seine
Arromanches-les-Bains
Bayeux ②
Ouistreham
Caen
CALVAD
Falai
Flers
ORNE
La Ferté-Macé

0 km    20
0 miles    20

### 5 Notre-Dame, Rouen

It took nearly 400 years to build this splendid Gothic cathedral, from the beautifully harmonious nave to the ornately carved west front (see pp24–5).

### 6 Étretat

The cliffs of the Côte d'Albâtre are at their most stunning around this seaside resort, which has a collection of handsome medieval buildings (see pp30–31).

### 7 Deauville and La Côte Fleurie

The resorts along this lovely stretch of coastline constitute a glamorous summer paradise (see pp32–3).

### 8 D-Day Beaches

The Allied landings and the Battle of Normandy in 1944 are commemorated in museums, memorials and cemeteries throughout the area (see pp34–7).

### 9 Pays d'Auge

Quintessential Normandy, this area is famous for its cider, cheese, gently rolling landscapes, orchards, and half-timbered manor houses (see pp38–9).

### 10 Fondation Claude Monet, Giverny

The house where Monet lived for more than 40 years, and his stunning garden, are a tribute to the painter (see pp40–43).

# TOP 10 ⭐ Mont-St-Michel

One of the most spectacular sights in Normandy, this craggy rock crowned by a magnificent abbey appears to erupt from the surrounding landscape – a broad expanse of sand or sea, depending on the dramatic tides. The region's star attraction since pilgrims first flocked here 1,000 years ago, it now draws some three million visitors each year – and has perhaps 50 true inhabitants.

### 1 Abbey

This splendid building (right) is a pleasing jumble of architectural styles. Its jewel is the Merveille, built during the abbey's heyday and incorporating cloisters, the knights' hall, the refectory and the guests' room.

### 2 Ramparts

Punctuated by imposing towers (right), the longest section was built to repel the English during the Hundred Years' War. The abbot's soldiers lodged in the Tour de l'Arcade.

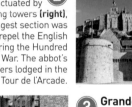

### 3 Grande Rue

Through the fortified Porte du Roy, its portcullis still visible, the Grande Rue (left) winds steeply uphill. This pretty, narrow cobbled street was the original route used by pilgrims in the 12th century, and is still the way to the top of the Mont. These days, however, visitors have to run the gauntlet of souvenir shops and overpriced restaurants.

### AN ISLAND

Mont-St-Michel has become an island again for the first time in more than a hundred years. As part of a major project aimed at restoring the "maritime character" of the Mont, the unsightly causeway that used to link the island to the mainland has been removed and a new wooden bridge has been built. This has allowed the tidal waters to flow freely, removing many years' build-up of silt and sand. Visitors can no longer drive right up to the Mont, and have to leave their cars on the mainland. You can cross the bridge on foot, by bike or by bus.

**Map of Mont-St-Michel**

✈ 4 5 km (3 miles)
✈ 8 15 km (9 miles)

### 4 Scriptorial d'Avranches
Films and games lead visitors through a celebration of the written word, from illuminated medieval manuscripts **(above)** to ebooks.

### 5 Archéoscope
A large model of the Mont rises from a huge tank of water in a spectacle of sound and light, with a historical commentary in English.

### 6 Église St-Pierre
The parish church, begun in the 11th century but not completed until the 17th, has an apse that straddles a narrow street. Its treasures include a silver statue of St Michael.

### 7 Chapelle St-Aubert
Legend tells of a huge rock blocking the entrance to a cave where the abbey now stands. Nobody could move it until a small boy miraculously pushed it into the sea with his foot. This tiny 15th-century chapel **(right)** occupies the site where the rock was supposed to have landed.

### 8 Ecomusée de la Baie du Mont Saint-Michel
This child-friendly exploration centre on the coast has models and interactive displays about the environment and wildlife of the bay, along with its history of fishing and salt production.

### 9 Logis Tiphaine
The chief of the king's armies Bertrand du Guesclin built this house in 1365 for his wife Tiphaine as a safe haven while he was away at war.

### 10 Musée Historique
Highlights are the garden periscope, a medieval monks' bath, 17th-century riding boots, and a re-creation of the abbey's prison cells.

**NEED TO KNOW**

**MAP B5** ■ Office de Tourisme: bd de l'Avancée ■ 02 33 60 14 30
*Abbey:* 02 33 89 80 00; May–Aug: 9am–7pm; Sep–Apr: 9:30am–6pm. Adm charge
*Musée Historique:* 02 33 60 07 01; 9am–6pm daily. Adm charge
*Logis Tiphaine:* 02 33 60 23 34; Mid-Feb–mid-Nov:

9am–6pm daily. Adm charge
*Archéoscope:* 02 33 89 01 85; Mid-Feb–Jun & Sep–mid-Nov: 9:30am–5:30pm; Jul–Aug: 9am–6pm. Adm charge
*Scriptorial d'Avranches:* pl d'Estouteville, Avranches; 02 33 79 57 00; Apr–Jun & Sep: 10am–1pm & 2–6pm Tue–Sun; Jul–Aug: 10am–1pm & 2–7pm Tue–Sun; Oct–Dec & Feb–Mar: 2–6pm Tue–Sat. Adm charge

*Ecomusée de la Baie du Mont Saint-Michel:* rte de Grouin de Sud, Vains; 02 33 89 06 06; Apr–Jun: 2–6pm; Jul–Aug: 10am–7pm. Sep: 10am–6pm. Adm charge

■ Cafés and restaurants line the Grande Rue.
■ Call Chemins de la Baie (02 33 89 80 88) for a guided walk of the Bay of Mont-St-Michel.

# Mont-St-Michel: Abbey Features

### 1 West Terrace
From this terrace, there are breathtaking views over the bay. On a clear day, you can see as far as the Channel Islands – the source of the granite used to build the abbey.

**Key to Floorplan**
■ Church level
■ Middle level

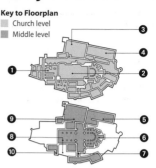

**Chancel interior in the Abbey Church**

### 2 Abbey Church
Despite its fine roof, the austere Romanesque nave – the oldest part of the church – is eclipsed by the fine Flamboyant Gothic chancel. The walls on the west front are scorched from a fire that broke out in the 19th century, when the abbey was used as a prison.

### 3 Cloisters
A garden enclosed by a double row of delicate pink granite columns, the cloisters gave the monks a place to meditate, converse and exercise.

### 4 Refectory
Apart from one monk, who would read aloud from the Scriptures, the monks ate in silence in this room, which has rows of narrow side windows invisible from the entrance.

### 5 Guests' Room
Light floods through large windows into this elegant rib-vaulted room, which was used for receiving important guests. Food was cooked in the two huge fireplaces.

### 6 Crypt of the Mighty Pillars
To support the new chancel, ten granite pillars were built in 1446 in this crypt, a room for those awaiting the judgment of the abbot, who presided over the courtroom next door.

### 7 St Martin's Crypt
Decorated with frescoes, this crypt, which provided the foundation for the south transept, was the funeral chapel for lay people.

### 8 Prison
During the French Revolution, the abbey began to be used as a prison. The iron cage used to confine dangerous prisoners is long gone, but the vast wheel for hoisting up provisions is still in place.

### 9 Knights' Hall
This vast, imposing hall was the monks' *scriptorium*, where they studied and copied manuscripts. A wooden trap door led to the food store.

**The Gothic vaults of the Knight's Hall**

### 10 St Etienne's Chapel
The monks' funeral chapel was well placed between the infirmary and the ossuary, where the bones of the dead were preserved. Monks kept vigil over the dead for three days and three nights.

## ST MICHAEL AND ST AUBERT

According to legend, St Michael, the archangel, appeared three times in a dream to Aubert, Bishop of Avranches, commanding him to build an oratory on Mont Tombe (tomb on the hill). When Aubert delayed, the impatient archangel prodded a finger into Aubert's forehead, leaving a dent. Aubert built a small church in 708, which rapidly became a centre of pilgrimage for the *miquelots*, followers of the cult of St Michael, which had taken root in the West in the 5th century. The brightly gilded statue on top of the abbey spire, sculpted in 1897 by Emmanuel Frémiet, portrays the archangel in traditional, warlike fashion. Armour-clad, he is slaying a dragon (the symbol of the Devil) with his sword. In his other hand he carries a set of scales. This is a reference to the medieval belief that it was his role to weigh the souls on Judgment Day.

**Frémiet's statue of St Michael on the abbey spire**

**TOP 10 EVENTS IN THE HISTORY OF MONT-ST-MICHEL**

**1** 708: Aubert, Bishop of Avranches, builds an oratory on Mont Tombe

**2** 966: Duke Richard I imposes Benedictine rule

**3** 1017: work on Romanesque abbey church begins; village grows up below

**4** 1434: ramparts completed during Hundred Years' War

**5** 1789: monks leave; abbey converted to a political prison during the French Revolution

**6** 1874: becomes a Historic Monument and opens to the public

**7** 1877: construction of causeway connecting the Mont and the mainland

**8** 1969: Benedictine monks return and leave again in 2001

**9** 1979: UNESCO designates Mont-St-Michel a World Heritage Site

**10** 2014: footbridge linking the Mont to the mainland completed, and opened to the public on 22 July

**The archangel Michael** is the warlike angel of the Apocalypse who slays the Devil – in the form of a dragon – in the great conflict at the end of time. He is the patron saint of mariners in Normandy.

# TOP 10 ⭐ Bayeux Tapestry

Both a unique historical document and an astonishing work of art, the Bayeux Tapestry tells the story of the Norman Conquest of England in 1066 – and it does so with thrilling narrative drive. Stitched in eight brilliant shades of red, yellow and blue wool, the 58 strip-cartoon-style scenes were embroidered just 11 years after the Conquest onto a single 70-m (230-ft) long linen cloth – at the behest, it is thought, of William the Conquerer's half-brother Odo, Bishop of Bayeux. It is displayed in a renovated seminary, along with helpful explanatory exhibitions and an excellent audio guide.

### 1 The Tapestry

The tapestry is displayed unfurled in a horseshoe-shaped gallery **(above)**, with dim lighting to preserve its colours. The audio guide describes each scene, adding detail about the lifestyle of the period.

### 2 Harold's Mission to Normandy

In the first scene **(left)**, Edward the Confessor is seen sending Harold from England to Normandy to tell Duke William that he will succeed to the English throne. Harold sets off for the coast.

### 4 William Invades England

As soon as William has ordered his invasion fleet to be built (No. 35) **(above)**, the stylized trees that serve to break the tapestry's scenes cease to appear, and the story gathers pace.

### 3 The Tapestry Explained

Echoing the tapestry, an 85-m (280-ft) band of cloth explains the story. An English translation of the Latin text is shown beside images of each scene.

### 5 The Film

Maps and drawings depict the events of the Norman Conquest, and a film tells the story from the perspective of William's half-brother, Bishop Odo.

### 6 Harold's Oath
This critical scene (No. 27) provides the moral impetus for the story, told from the Norman point of view: Harold, touching holy relics, swears his allegiance to Duke William **(above)**.

### 7 The England of William
Using life-size figures, maps and scale models (including a delightful model of a village in Hampshire, England), William's influence on every sphere of English life after his conquest is cleverly portrayed.

### 8 Harold's Perjury
Harold returns to England from Normandy. On the death of Edward the Confessor, he is crowned king, breaking his oath to William. The appearance of Halley's Comet foretells his doom (No. 32).

### 9 The Battle of Hastings
The battle scenes **(below)** are marvellously depicted – full of the clash, clamour and bloody horror of medieval warfare (Nos. 51–58).

### 10 The Death of Harold
The tapestry comes to an abrupt end with the death of Harold and the victory of William over the English. The scene seems to support the legend that Harold was shot in the eye with an arrow.

**NEED TO KNOW**

**MAP D3** ■ Office du Tourisme: pont St-Jean; 02 31 51 28 28 ■ Centre Guillaume-le-Conquérant: rue de Nesmond; 02 31 51 25 50.

**Open** May–Aug: 9am–6:15pm; Mar–Apr, Sep–Oct: 9am–5:45pm; Nov–Feb 9:30am–12:30pm, 2–5:15pm daily. Closed 3 weeks early Jan.

Adm: €9, concessions €4; under-10s free

■ For an excellent lunch, try Le Pommier, rue des Cuisiniers, or Le P'tit Resto, 2 rue du Bienvenu.

■ In July and August, the tourist office runs guided tours of the cathedral (€5) twice a day. The tours include the treasury room and the chapter house.

**Museum Guide**
The visit to the tapestry itself takes about 30 minutes: a slow-moving walkway takes you past the 58 tapestry scenes, with commentary in English for adults and children from the audio guides provided. Afterwards, a film and exhibition provide interesting background information on the story of the Norman Conquest and the tapestry.

# Sights in Bayeux

### 1 Musée d'Art et d'Histoire Baron Gérard

137 rue du Bienvenu ■ 02 31 92 14 21 ■ Open daily May–Sep: 9:30am–6:30pm; mid-Feb–Apr, Oct–Dec: 10am–12:30pm, 2–6pm ■ Adm charge

Set in the medieval Episcopal palace, MAHB traces Bayeux's history through prehistoric finds, paintings, porcelain and lace. Highlights include a frescoed chapel.

**Bayeux's Cathédrale Notre-Dame**

### 2 Cathédrale Notre-Dame

Much altered over the centuries, the cathedral was consecrated in the presence of William the Conqueror in 1077.

### 3 Musée Mémorial de la Bataille de Normandie

Bayeux is the perfect base for visits to the D-Day beaches. This museum provides an excellent chronological introduction to the Battle of Normandy for all the family (see p36).

### 4 Conservatoire de la Dentelle

Maison Adam et Eve, 2 rue du Bienvenu ■ Open 10am–12:30pm, 2–6pm Mon–Sat (closes 5pm Mon & Thu)

Visitors can enjoy watching a group of dedicated craftswomen at work as they continue the tradition of intricate Bayeux lacemaking.

### 5 British Cemetery and Memorial

The largest British war cemetery in Normandy contains 4,144 graves.

**Map of Bayeux**

### 6 The River Aure

The banks of the River Aure supported many trades in the Middle Ages, including millers, tanners and dyers. A river path offers glimpses of this prosperous era, and passes through parks and play areas.

### 7 Le P'tit Train

From the cathedral and tourist office ■ 02 97 56 67 46 ■ Apr–Sep: several times daily ■ Adm charge

Discover the history and monuments of Vieux Bayeux during a 35-minute trip aboard the Little Train.

### 8 Jardin Public de Bayeux

55 rte de Port-en-Bessin ■ Open daily Apr–Nov: 9am–8pm; Sep–Apr: 9am–5pm

A botanical garden with a weeping beech tree 13 m (40 ft) in diameter.

### 9 Le Mémorial des Reporters

Liberty Alley ■ 02 31 51 28 28

This memorial garden has 27 stone pillars inscribed with the names of over 2,000 journalists who have died covering conflicts since 1945.

### 10 Vieux Bayeux

Follow the way-marked route round the streets of old Bayeux, with information posts at points of interest.

**Medieval Bayeux**

## WILLIAM THE CONQUEROR

A warrior through and through, William, Duke of Normandy and King of England, lived and died by the sword. Yet despite his appetite for battle (the Bayeux Tapestry illustrates some of his forays in Normandy), he had a statesmanlike ability to create order out of chaos. Having won the English crown, he made radical changes and improvements to society by fusing continental practices with native customs – in particular, instituting a type of feudalism that strengthened the monarchy, restrained the power of the Church, and supported the educational system of the day. With his wife Matilda, he founded some 30 abbeys, including the two at Caen *(see pp52–3)*.

**The Domesday Book**, a huge and detailed record of English land ownership at the close of the 11th century, set the seal on Norman land reforms – and the occupation. It is now regarded as one of the most important documents in English history.

**Manuscript depicting William the Conqueror**

**TOP 10
EVENTS IN WILLIAM'S LIFE**

**1** 1027: Born in Falaise

**2** 1035: Receives the Duchy of Normandy on his father's death

**3** 1047: Helped by King Henri I of France, William crushes rebel barons in Normandy

**4** 1051: Edward the Confessor, his cousin, purportedly promises him the English throne

**5** 1064: Harold Godwinson – rival heir to the English throne – swears allegiance to William, perhaps through trickery or under duress

**6** 1066: Harold succeeds Edward as king of England

**7** 1066: William invades England, defeats Harold, and is crowned king at Westminster Abbey on Christmas Day

**8** 1072: Ruthlessly crushes all rebellions until England is conquered and united

**9** 1086: Commissions the Domesday Book, an invaluable survey of land ownership

**10** 1087: Dies in Rouen from a battle wound

# TOP 10 ⭐ Honfleur

Seductively pretty, with cobbled streets and half-timbered or slate-fronted houses, Honfleur is a working port with a long maritime history. First mentioned in documents of the 11th century, by the 15th century it had become a significant fortified port. Its heyday came some 200 years later, when it spawned intrepid explorers like Samuel de Champlain, who set out from here to found Quebec. Le Vieux Bassin, the charming old dock at the heart of the town, is brimming with colourful sailing boats; artists have flocked here since the 19th century.

### 1 Le Vieux Bassin

This picturesque harbour (below) was built in the 17th century at the behest of Colbert, Louis XIV's chief finance minister, who also ordered the demolition of the ramparts. Quai Ste-Catherine is particularly attractive.

### 2 Musée Eugène Boudin

Now housing an exciting collection of 19th- and 20th-century art, the museum (below) was founded in 1868 by Honfleur's best-known artists, Boudin and Louis-Alexandre Dubourg.

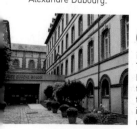

### 3 Église Ste-Catherine

Built to replace a church destroyed in the Hundred Years' War, the largest wooden church in France (right) is half-timbered inside and out, with twin naves and tall oak pillars. The heavy bells required a separate stone bell tower.

### 4 Greniers à Sel

Larger cod catches in the late 16th century increased the demand for salt as a preservative. To accommodate this, two huge salt stores were built in the main street of the *enclos*, the walled town. Stone from the old ramparts was used for the walls, and oak for the roofs – which are still in superb condition. Now they are used for meetings, conferences, exhibitions and concerts.

**Map of Honfleur**

### ⑤ Église St-Léonard
From its 16th-century Flamboyant door to its 18th-century octagonal bell tower, St-Léonard is a hotchpotch of styles. The unusual copper lectern was produced in Villedieu-les-Poêles *(see p104)*.

### ⑥ Musée de la Marine
Housed in a 14th century church, the Musée de la Marine **(above)** traces the history of the port through scale models, instruments, engravings, cutlasses, cannons and other fascinating artifacts.

### ⑦ Musée d'Ethnographie
Nine rooms crammed with objects, furniture and costumes transport you back through the centuries. The most delightful part is the haberdasher's shop, complete with ribbon samples.

### ⑧ Les Maisons Satie
A suitably offbeat tribute to the eccentric composer Erik Satie, born here in 1866. Videos, surreal room sets and life-size electronic sculptures re-create his fantasy world.

### ⑨ Chapelle Notre-Dame de Grâce
Explorers came to this enchanting little chapel **(right)** to pray before setting sail. Built in the early 17th century to replace a chapel that fell into the sea, it remains a place of pilgrimage.

### ⑩ Pont de Normandie
Opened in 1995, this elegant space-age bridge links Honfleur and Le Havre. Its 856-m (2,800-ft) span held the record – albeit briefly – for the world's longest cable-stayed bridge.

**NEED TO KNOW**

**MAP F3** ■ Office du Tourisme: quai Lepaulmier; 02 31 89 23 30

*Musée Eugène Boudin:* pl Erik Satie. Mid-Mar–Sep: 10am–noon & 2–6pm Wed–Mon; Oct–Dec & mid-Feb–mid-Mar: 2:30–5:30pm Mon & Wed–Fri, 10am–noon & 2:30–5:30pm Sat & Sun. Adm charge

*Musée de la Marine/Musée d'Ethnographie:* rue de la Prison, off quai St-Etienne. Mid-Feb–Mar & Oct–mid-Nov: 2:30–5:30pm Tue–Fri, 10am–noon & 2:30–5:30pm Sat & Sun; Apr–Sep: 10am–noon & 2–6:30pm Tue–Sun. Adm charge

*Les Maisons Satie:* 67 bd Charles V. Mid-Feb–Apr & Oct–Dec: 11am–6pm Wed–Mon; May–Sep: 10am–7pm Wed–Mon. Closed Jan–mid-Feb. Adm charge

■ In summer, enjoy a coffee at one of the pavement cafés in Le Vieux Bassin.

■ Audio guides can be hired for €5 from the tourist office.

# TOP 10 ★ Abbaye de Jumièges

The hauntingly beautiful, bleached white ruins of this Benedictine abbey stand in a loop of the Seine. Founded by St Philibert in 654, following the donation of the estate to him by Queen Bathilde, wife of Clovis II, it was one of a number of abbeys built under the dukes of Normandy as the region turned to Christianity. Despite its chequered history (sacked by Vikings, it was rebuilt only to later be reduced to ruins and used as a quarry), it is a part of Normandy's rich heritage and an important stop on the famous Abbey Route.

### 1 Notre-Dame's West Façade
Stark and simple, Notre-Dame's impressive Romanesque west façade (above) was built around 1060, with a projecting porch flanked by two massive towers. Square at the base, octagonal above, they originally had wooden spires.

### 2 Storeroom
Once a welcoming hall for important guests, the storeroom, Gothic in design, Romanesque in decoration, is intact but for its ribbed vaulting.

**The Abbey Grounds**

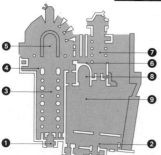

### 3 Notre-Dame's Nave
Only the walls of Normandy's tallest Romanesque nave (above) still stand, left open to the skies after the demolition of the plaster vault that replaced the original wooden ceiling.

### 4 Notre-Dame's Transept
The west wall is all that survives of the 11th-century transept. The transept crossing was topped by a lantern tower, to let in the maximum amount of light in poor weather.

**THE MAURISTS**
After a period of spiritual decline in the 16th and 17th centuries, the Maurists, a fiercely intellectual and devout congregation of St Maur, founded in Paris in 1618, were dispatched to reform Jumièges Abbey. Among their improvements to its physical structure were a vast library, the abbey dwelling-house, and a monumental double staircase leading to a broad terrace and the gardens beyond.

**(5) Notre-Dame's Choir**
Nothing remains of the earliest choir. The ruins **(above)** are from a 13th-century Gothic version, comprising an ambulatory with seven radiating chapels. An ornate rood screen is decorated with bas-reliefs illustrating the Passion of Christ.

**(6) Charles VII's Passage**
This covered arcade, built in the early 1330s to link the two churches, predates Charles VII, but was named after a visit he made here with his mistress, Agnès Sorel, whose heart is buried under a marble slab in the north transept chapel.

**Église St-Pierre (7)**
The western section of this church **(right)** was built in the first few decades of the 9th century, before the Viking raids on Jumièges. It is an important monument of the Carolingian period.

**(8) Chapterhouse**
It was in this 11th- to 12th-century hall that a chapter from the rules of St Benedict was read out every morning, and monastic affairs were discussed. Between the 12th and mid-13th centuries, it became the abbots' burial ground.

**(9) Cloister**
Today, the cloister **(left)** is an expanse of grass with a yew tree at its centre, but it was once the heart of the abbey, used by the monks for promenades, ceremonies, meditation and processions.

**(10) Abbey Dwelling-House**
Northeast of the abbey ruins, this grand house **(below)** was built for François de Harlay de Champvallon, a "commendatory" abbot who was appointed directly by the king.

**NEED TO KNOW**
MAP G3 ■ 24 rue Guillaume-le-Conquérant, 76480 Jumièges ■ 02 35 37 24 02 ■ www.abbayedejumieges.fr

**Open** mid-Apr–mid-Sep: 9:30am–6:30pm daily; mid-Sep–mid-Apr and Easter: 10am–12:30pm; 2:30–5pm. Closed 1 Jan, 1 May, 1 Nov, 11 Nov, 25 Dec

Adm: adults €6.50; 18–25-year-olds €4; children under 18 free

■ Stop for lunch at the Auberge des Ruines (pl de la Mairie), opposite the abbey entrance.

■ For €5 you can hire tablets with an audiovisual guide in English. This includes 3-D reconstructions of the abbey using augmented reality.

# TOP 10 ★ Cathédrale Notre-Dame, Rouen

Located in the historic heart of the city, this magnificent cathedral took nearly 400 years to build. It stands as a record of the entire span of French Gothic architecture. Through the centuries, it has captured the imagination of artists, most famously Monet, who painted the west façade 30 times between 1892 and 1894 – at different times of day and year, and in various weather conditions, in order to capture the subtle changes of colour and light. His thick impasto suggests the texture of ornately carved stone.

### 1 West Façade
Familiar through Monet's paintings, this richly sculpted façade **(above)** reflects the evolution of the Gothic style. The most elaborate part is Roulland le Roux's early 16th-century central porch.

### 2 Booksellers' Courtyard
Created as a short cut for the local canons, this narrow courtyard is notable for the intricacy of its carvings.

**Floorplan of Cathédrale Notre-Dame**

### 3 Spire
Writer Gustave Flaubert was famously rude about it, but the people of Rouen have grown fond of this cast-iron spire **(above)**, the tallest in France. A bold 19th-century design, it matches the height of the hills surrounding the city.

### 4 Nave
Typical of the early Gothic style, the exquisitely proportioned nave **(right)** has four storeys: arches, tribunes (in this case, false ones), a gallery and upper windows.

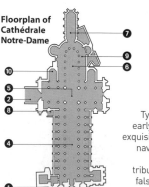

### 5 Lantern Tower
The tower rises a breathtaking 151 m (495 ft) above the transept crossing from floor to keystone, flooding the interior with light. At the base of each of its columns, busts 1 m (3 ft) high, said to represent the tower's builders, appear to be shouldering its weight.

### 6 Choir
The 13th-century choir is half-circled by tall pillars with vast carved capitals supporting pointed arches. The choir stalls, which are from the same period, are carved with comic scenes.

### 7 Lady Chapel
The delicate 14th-century Lady Chapel contains the tombs of more than 150 dignitaries, including the Tomb of the Cardinals of Amboise by le Roux.

### 8 Library Staircase
The lower two flights of this superb staircase **(right)** are the work of Guillaume Pontifs, while the upper two are 18th-century copies. The ogee arch above the wrought-iron door is typical Flamboyant Gothic.

**THE HISTORY OF THE CATHEDRAL**

Building started in the mid-12th century on the site of two earlier cathedrals: the first, 4th-century; the second, an 11th-century Romanesque building from which the crypt survives. After a fire in 1200, work continued on the present building into the 16th century. Having survived the next four centuries more or less intact, it was devastated by bombing on 19 April 1944; only two flying buttresses prevented the whole building from collapsing. Repairs continue to the present day.

### 9 Ambulatory Tombs
Here are effigies of Rollo, William Long Sword (known for his short stature rather than the length of his sword), and Richard the Lionheart, who ordered that his heart be buried in Rouen cathedral *(see p47)*.

### 10 Window of St Julian the Hospitaller
In jewel-like blues and reds, this early 13th-century stained-glass window tells the tragic story of St Julian, who accidentally murdered his parents and founded a hospital in penance.

**NEED TO KNOW**

**MAP M6** ■ pl de la Cathédrale, 76000 Rouen ■ 02 35 71 85 65

**Open** Apr–Oct: 9am–7pm Mon–Sat & 8am–6pm Sun; Nov–Mar: 9am–noon & 2–6pm Mon–Sat, 2–6pm Sun. Closed Mon am

■ Guided tours at 2:30pm Sat & Sun (daily in French school hols & Jul–mid-Sep)

■ In a half-timbered building near the cathedral's north front, Dame Cakes (70 rue St-Romain) has excellent tarts and gâteaux.

■ You can get a good view of the famous west façade from the tourist office (25 pl de la Cathédrale).

■ Albane Courtyard reopened in 2012 after excavations, which uncovered relics of earlier cathedrals.

# Other Sights in Rouen

**Courtyard of Musée des Beaux-Arts**

### 1 Musée des Beaux-Arts
MAP M5 ■ Espl Marcel Duchamp ■ Open 10am–6pm Wed–Mon

Highlights include paintings by Caravaggio, Velázquez, Monet, Géricault, Dufy and Modigliani.

### 2 Aître St-Maclou
MAP N6 ■ 186 rue Martainville (at end of passage) ■ Open 9am–6pm daily

This tranquil 14th-century courtyard was a plague cemetery. The timbered galleries are decorated with *memento mori* motifs.

### 3 Église St-Maclou
MAP N6 ■ Pl Barthélémy ■ Open 10am–5:30pm Sat & Sun

A masterpiece of the Flamboyant style of Gothic architecture.

**The vaults of Église St-Maclou**

### 4 Le Gros Horloge
MAP L5 ■ 191 rue du Gros Horloge ■ Open Tue–Sun ■ Adm charge

Moved from the Gothic belfry to an arch in 1527, the Great Clock has two dials, a single hour hand and a panel showing the phases of the moon.

### 5 Église Ste-Jeanne d'Arc
MAP L5 ■ Pl du Vieux Marché ■ Open 10am–noon, 2–6pm Mon–Thu & Sat, 2–6pm Fri & Sun

The cross outside this modern church marks the site of Joan's martyrdom.

### 6 Musée National de l'Éducation
MAP N5 ■ 185 rue Eau-de-Robec ■ Open 1:30–6:15pm Mon & Wed–Fri, 10am–12:30pm & 1:30–6:15pm Sat & Sun ■ Adm charge

This small museum charts 500 years of children's education.

### 7 Palais de Justice
MAP M5 ■ 36 rue aux Juifs ■ Closed to the public

The ornate law courts are a magnificent example of late medieval Gothic architecture.

**Façade of the Palais de Justice**

### 8 Historial Jeanne d'Arc
MAP M5 ■ 7 rue St-Romain ■ Open 9:45am–7:45pm Tue–Sun (Jun–Sep: to 8:45pm Fri & Sat) ■ Adm charge

Multimedia displays trace the story of Joan of Arc in the archbishop's palace where she was sentenced.

### 9 Musée Le Secq des Tournelles
MAP M5 ■ 2 rue Jacques Villon ■ Open 2–6pm Wed–Mon

The world's largest collection of historic wrought-ironware.

### 10 Musée de la Céramique
MAP M4 ■ 1 rue Faucon ■ Open 2–6pm Wed–Mon

More than 6,000 pieces chart the history of Rouen's earthenware.

## JOAN OF ARC

Although the facts of Joan's life are well recorded, she remains an enigma. The Maid of Orléans, as she came to be known, was from a pious peasant family, could barely read or write, yet succeeded in persuading the Dauphin to let her lead his army. The image of the androgynous, armour-clad Joan is iconic, portrayed through the centuries by sculptors, painters, playwrights and film-makers. She clearly had conviction and charisma, but did the "voices" she heard throughout her short life make her a visionary or a schizophrenic? After her canonization, France adopted Joan as its

patron saint, and her feast day (30 May) is celebrated throughout the country.

**Joan of Arc's execution** was meant to take place on 24 May 1431, but at the last moment she broke down and recanted. She later retracted that recantation, and met her fate on 30 May.

**TOP 10 EVENTS IN JOAN OF ARC'S LIFE**

**1** Born in Domrémy on 6 January 1412

**2** Aged 13, hears voices for the first time

**3** Four years later, the voices tell her to save France from the English

**4** Gains an audience with Dauphin Charles on 9 March 1429

**5** Leads the French to victory at Orléans (8 May); Charles' coronation follows (17 July)

**6** Captured by the Burgundians in May 1430; they sell her to the English

**7** Tried in Rouen for heresy and witchcraft, 21 February to 23 May 1431

**8** Burned at the stake in place du Vieux Marché on 30 May 1431

**9** Rehabilitated in 1456

**10** Canonized in 1920

**Painting depicting Joan of Arc entering Orléans in May 1429**

***Following pages*** *Mont-St-Michel*

# TOP 10 ★ Étretat

Étretat, once a fishing village and then a popular seaside resort in the 19th century, is arguably Normandy's most alluring coastal town. Located on the Côte d'Albâtre (Alabaster Coast), it is flanked by two spectacular cliffs, the Falaise d'Aval and the Falaise d'Amont, each one hollowed out by the sea to form dramatic arches. Artists such as Courbet and Monet were beguiled by the play of light on these white cliffs and captured them many times on canvas.

### 1 Esplanade

Étretat has no port, just a restaurant-lined esplanade, curving along the seafront and affording picture-postcard views of the dramatic cliff formations to either side. If you come here for a stroll at dusk, you can see the cliffs spectacularly lit up.

### 2 Memorial to the Aviators Nungesser and Coli

Atop the Falaise d'Amont is a monument to French aviators Nungesser and Coli **(above)**, who left Paris in 1927, hoping to make the first ever transatlantic flight. They never made it and were last seen over Étretat.

### 3 Porte d'Amont

Sculpted into the Falaise d'Amont, the cliff on Étretat's northeastern side, this natural archway was likened to an elephant dipping its trunk into the water by the author Guy de Maupassant. When the tide is out, you can walk along the beach almost to the foot of the arch.

### 4 Notre-Dame de la Garde

Perched on the edge of the Falaise d'Amont and with sweeping views out to sea, this mariners' chapel **(right)**, originally dating from 1856, was destroyed in World War II and rebuilt in 1950.

### 5 Falaise d'Aval

On the south-western side of Étretat lies the Falaise d'Aval, with its natural waterfront arch **(above)**. From the clifftop here, admire the "aiguille d'Étretat", a natural "needle" of rock rearing up out of the water.

**Map of Étretat**

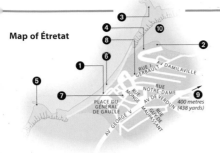

### 6 Beach
Étretat's shingle beach **(below)** slopes steeply into the water. Wooden boats were once hauled up the beach to serve as bars in summer. Now some have been thatched over to become permanent restaurants.

### 7 Place Foch
The market square has some attractive half-timbered medieval buildings and a picturesque wooden market hall **(above)**, which houses souvenir shops. Stalls are set up in the square every Thursday.

### NEED TO KNOW

**MAP F2** ■ Office de Tourisme: pl Maurice Guillard ■ 02 35 27 05 21 ■ www.etretat.net

*Parc des Roches:* rue Jules Gerbeau; 02 35 29 80 59; Jul & Aug: 1–7pm daily, Apr–Jun, Sep & Oct: 2–6pm Wed, Sat & Sun. Adm to mini-golf: €3.50, children €2.50

*Vélo-Rail:* La Gare, Les Loges; 02 35 29 49 61; www.lafrancevuedurail.fr/ttepac; Jul & Aug: daily, Mar–Jun & Sep–Nov: Wed, Sat & Sun. Adm: from €27

■ The picturesque paths up to the clifftops are very steep and have no railings, so take extra care.

■ Keen golfers should check out Étretat's golf course. High up on the cliffs, it is one of the most spectacularly sited in France.

### 8 Belle Époque Villas
Étretat sports a number of grand houses, among them the Villa Orphée, built for composer Jacques Offenbach, and La Guillette, where Maupassant lived for a time.

### 9 Vélo-Rail Les Loges– Étretat
For a fun outing, cycle the 5-km (3-mile) railway track from Les Loges to Étretat in a pedal-powered vehicle, and return in an old diesel train.

### 10 Parc des Roches
Set atop the Falaise d'Amont, the Parc des Roches leisure park has a paddling pool for children, slides, a bouncy castle and miniature golf. Grown-ups can relax enjoying the panoramic views out to sea.

# TOP 10 ⭐ Deauville and La Côte Fleurie

Between Honfleur and Cabourg, the Norman coastline becomes a playground of resorts, casinos, water sports, sunshine and sandy beaches backed by wooded hills. It all started in Trouville, which triggered the 19th-century rage for sea bathing. Next came racy, romantic Deauville – created in the 1860s by a trio of wealthy entrepreneurs, and embellished in 1910 with a boardwalk, casino and racecourse. In contrast, Touques and Dives-sur-Mer have historic links with William the Conqueror, while stately Cabourg will be forever associated with Marcel Proust.

## 1 Deauville

Racehorses pounding the beach at sunrise, a glamorous wooden boardwalk, the glittering casino, the sumptuous Hôtel Normandy, the Bar du Soleil, the Pompeian Baths, designer shops, marinas, extravagant mock-Tudor villas **(above)**: this is the epitome of an up-market seaside resort.

## 2 Touques

The vestiges of William the Conqueror's castle can be visited at Bonneville, above the port of Touques. In the neat town centre stands the 11th-century church of St-Pierre, with its unusual octagonal lantern.

## 3 Trouville-sur-Mer

In contrast to its neighbour Deauville, the town of Trouville **(below)** exudes a happy-go-lucky air. Attractions include its south-facing waterfront boulevard, trawlers and fish market, children's amusements and the wonderfully florid 1912 casino and town hall.

### 4 Villers-sur-Mer
This resort **(above)** is the starting point of the Vaches Noires cliffs, where many fossils have been found. The Paléospace l'Odyssée museum is devoted to these finds.

### 5 Villerville
In the summer months, this seaside town, surrounded by woods and meadows, organizes long nature walks along the coast.

### 6 Mont Canisy
Mont Canisy rises above Deauville, with views from Le Havre to the Orne; underground is a warren of German bunkers and tunnels.

### 7 Falaise des Vaches Noires
A walk at low tide between Villers and Houlgate takes you past the Vaches Noires cliffs.

**THE HIGH LIFE**

A nonstop round of film festivals, horse racing, yachting regattas, tennis and golf tournaments, international bridge championships, jazz, and vintage car rallies keeps Deauville buzzing all year. But it's the hectic 100-day summer season that brings the beautiful people out in force, staying at the Normandy, dining at Ciro's, shopping for Cartier, posing on Les Planches, gambling, racegoing, or sipping cocktails on their yachts. Elegant, snooty, moneyed, but not brash or flashy: that's Deauville.

### 8 Houlgate
Like Villers-sur-Mer, Houlgate is a family resort notable for its Neo-Norman architecture – all half-timbering, gables, turrets and towers.

### 10 Dives-sur-Mer
The former port from which William set sail to conquer England boasts a magnificent oak-framed market hall **(left)** *(see p76)* and the church of Notre-Dame, founded in 1067.

### 9 Cabourg
Take tea at the Grand Hôtel **(right)**, vividly described by Proust in *A la recherche du temps perdu* and, like Cabourg itself, still redolent of those genteel 19th-century days.

**NEED TO KNOW**
MAP E3 ■ Office du Tourisme: 112 rue Victor Hugo, Deauville; 02 31 14 40 00 ■ Office du Tourisme: Jardins de l'Hôtel de Ville, Cabourg; 02 31 91 20 00

*Paléospace l'Odyssée:* av Jean Moulin, Villers-sur-Mer; 02 31 81 77 60; Feb–Aug: 10am–6pm daily (to 7pm Jul–Aug), Sep: 10am–6pm Wed–Mon, Oct–Jan: limited opening. Adm: €7.90, children €5.40

■ In Deauville, Bar du Soleil on Les Planches and Bar de la Mer in the port are great for people-watching.
■ In Trouville, dine at one of the many waterfront restaurants, such as Les Vapeurs *(see p99)*.
■ Dress up to visit Deauville: it will make you feel the part.
■ Access to Deauville beach is free; its pretty, colourful parasols – folded in a way unique to the town – are, however, quite expensive to hire.

# TOP 10 ★ D-Day Beaches

On 6 June 1944, Nazi-occupied France was invaded by British, American, Commonwealth and Canadian troops, resulting in the country's liberation. The Allied landings on the beaches of the Seine Bay (still known by their wartime codenames) and the ferocious Battle of Normandy that followed are commemorated today through a moving mixture of museums, memorials and cemeteries. Beautifully maintained and presented with great clarity, they give visitors a fascinating insight into the historic events of that momentous summer.

## 1 Utah Beach and Ste-Mère-Eglise
Over 13,000 US paratroopers were dropped into the Cotentin marshland; the US 4th Division came ashore on Utah (above) and linked up with them.

## 2 La Pointe du Hoc
Preserved as it was at the end of fighting, this bleak headland was stormed by elite US Rangers using ropes and ladders to scale the cliff, with heavy casualties.

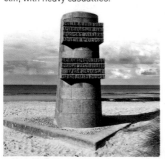

## 3 Omaha Beach
"Bloody Omaha" (above) saw terrible losses among the 1st and 29th US Divisions. A viewing table, two museums, 11 monuments and the American Cemetery tell the story.

## 4 Batteries de Longues
Longues-sur-Mer
Near Arromanches, this is the only German battery still to have its guns. Its observation post (above), on the edge of the cliff, can also be visited.

## 5 American Cemetery
Colleville-sur-Mer
Formal and serene, the world's most visited war cemetery (below) contains 9,387 graves, a moving memorial and exhibits explaining Operation Overlord.

### 6 Arromanches
The remains of the artificial Mulberry Harbour make a startling sight **(above)** – a testament to the ingenuity of Winston Churchill, who realized that if the troops wanted to land, they would have to bring their harbours with them.

**TOURING THE BEACHES**

Drivers can follow two themed and signposted routes, "Overlord – L'Assaut" and "D-Day – Le Choc", which are backed up by information "totems" at each place of interest (look for the dove symbol). The accompanying booklet (including a total of eight routes around Normandy), *The D-Day Landings and Battle of Normandy*, is available from local tourist offices, where you will also find details of recommended bus and taxi tour operators.

### 7 Gold Beach
Soon after landing here, the British 50th Division took Arromanches, and Mulberry Harbour was put in place.

### 8 Juno Beach
Several small seaside resorts line the beach assigned to the 3rd Canadian Division. A huge cross of Lorraine commemorates the triumphant return of General de Gaulle. The Canadian cemetery, at Beny-sur-Mer, is a beautiful spot containing 2,048 graves.

### 9 Sword Beach
Though the Allies established the beachhead with relative ease, the vital objective of Caen was thwarted, and its inhabitants had to wait another 34 days for their city to be liberated.

### 10 Pegasus Bridge
Bénouville/Ranville

The first Allies to land in France were the men of the British 6th Airborne Division, who seized this strategic bridge **(below)**, renamed after their insignia.

**NEED TO KNOW**

**MAP C3, D3** ■ Office du Tourisme: pont St-Jean, Bayeux; 02 31 51 28 28 ■ Observation bunker, La Pointe du Hoc: 10am–5pm daily.

■ La Marine at Arromanches, Le Marée at Grandcamp-Maisy and Le Bistrot d'à Côté at Port-en-Bessin *(see p99)* serve great seafood.

■ Select which museums, memorials and beaches you most want to see in advance. Perhaps start at the Musée de la Bataille de Normandie in Bayeux and end at Arromanches 360 *(see p36)*.

■ Tours are run by the Caen Memorial *(see p125)* and Normandy Tours (normandy-landing-tour.org).

# D-Day Museums

**Musée Mémorial de la Bataille**

### 1 Musée Mémorial de la Bataille de Normandie

MAP D3 ■ Bd Fabian-Ware, Bayeux ■ 02 31 51 46 90 ■ Open mid-Feb–Dec: daily ■ Adm charge

A good place to start, this museum gives a great overview of the battle.

### 2 Mémorial de la Liberté Retrouvée

MAP B2 ■ Quinéville ■ Open Apr–mid-Nov: daily ■ Adm charge ■ DA

This absorbing museum without weapons describes life in occupied France and the liberation of the Cotentin Peninsula.

### 3 Musée Airborne

MAP B3 ■ Ste-Mère-Eglise ■ Open Feb–Nov: daily ■ Adm charge

Shaped like a parachute, this museum commemorates the American paratroopers who were dropped behind Utah Beach.

### 4 D-Day Paratroopers Historical Center & Dead Man's Corner Museum

MAP B3 ■ Saint Côme du Mont ■ 02 33 23 61 95 ■ Open 9:30am–6pm daily ■ Adm charge ■ DA

A simulated flight in the Stoy Hora C47 plane and Eisenhower's flight jacket are highlights of this museum.

**Musée du Débarquement d'Utah-Beach**

### 5 Musée des Épaves

MAP C3 ■ Rte de Bayeux, Port-en-Bessin ■ 02 31 21 17 06 ■ Open May: Thu–Sun; Jun–Sep: daily; Oct: Sat & Sun ■ Adm charge

A fascinating collection of objects that have been recovered from wrecked warships on the seabed.

### 6 Musée du Débarquement

MAP D3 ■ Arromanches ■ Open Feb–Dec: daily ■ Adm charge

Built on the original site of Mulberry Harbour (see p35), this museum pays homage to the famous artificial ports.

### 7 Arromanches 360

MAP D3 ■ Arromanches ■ Open Feb–mid-Nov: daily; mid-Nov–Dec: Tue–Sun ■ Adm charge

Witness the events of D-Day in an extraordinary 18-minute film.

**Arromanches 360**

### 8 Juno Beach Centre

MAP D3 ■ Courseulles-sur-Mer ■ Open Feb–Dec: daily ■ Adm charge

A museum devoted to the Canadian Army's contribution to D-Day.

### 9 Musée Mémorial Pégasus

MAP E3, D3 ■ Ranville ■ Open Feb–mid-Dec: daily ■ Adm charge

A range of exhibits commemorate the British glider assault.

### 10 Musée du Débarquement d'Utah-Beach

MAP B3 ■ Ste-Marie du Mont ■ 02 33 71 53 35 ■ Open Jun–Sep 9:30am–7pm; Oct, Nov, Jan–May: 10am–6pm; ■ Adm charge ■ DA

Set on the beach where the US 4th Division landed on 6 June 1944, this museum recounts the events of the landing through numerous exhibits.

## OPERATION OVERLORD

The planning, manufacture of armaments, and training of men for the epic Allied invasion of Normandy in June 1944, codenamed Operation Overlord, began in earnest in the winter of 1943. D-Day was planned for 5 June, but was delayed for 24 hours due to bad weather. The unfavourable conditions, and an expected attack elsewhere (on Pas-de-Calais, nearer to Britain), caught the Germans by surprise when dawn brought the vast Allied fleet to the sandy beaches of the Seine Bay, flanked by airborne forces to the east and west. "It was as if every ship and every plane that had ever been built was there," said one British soldier. "The beach was alive with the shambles and the order of war … there were dead men and wounded men and men brewing tea."

Once beachheads were established on Utah, Omaha, Gold, Juno and Sword beaches, initial penetration into Normandy was uneven. Cherbourg fell on 26 June, Caen not until 9 July. Fighting conditions were grim among the hedgerows of Le Bocage (see p104), and it was not until 21 August, after the Germans were cornered in the Battle of the Falaise-Mortain Pocket, that the Battle of Normandy was finally won. Paris was liberated on 25 August.

**TOP 10**
## AMAZING D-DAY STATISTICS

1 4,000 ships in the fleet

2 5,800 bomber planes

3 4,900 fighter planes

4 153,000 Allied troops

5 20,000 vehicles

6 11,000 Allied forces casualties

7 2,500 dead

8 2,052,299 men came ashore following D-Day

9 3,098,259 tons of stores

10 640,000 Germans killed, wounded or taken prisoner in the Battle of Normandy

**A plane flies over the Normandy Beaches**

**Americans from the 1st US Infantry** land at Omaha Beach, the largest of the assault beaches, on D-Day, June 6 1944. In the first wave of attacks 2,400 died.

# 🔟 ⭐ Pays d'Auge

Apple and pear orchards, thatched farmhouses and half-timbered manor houses tucked into the hills, fat brown-and-white cows, producers selling cider and cheese – all these and more can be found in the Pays d'Auge. Stretching north to La Côte Fleurie *(see pp32–3)*, and bisected by the River Touques, the region perfectly encapsulates the charms of Normandy. Top attractions include villages, châteaux and abbeys – and of course, a Camembert museum and a Calvados distillery.

### Lisieux ①

The region's principal town is connected with St Thérèse, who achieved posthumous renown for her book *Histoire d'une âme* (Story of a Soul), and was canonized in 1925. More than two million people visit the Basilique Ste Thérèse **(right)** annually, making it the second largest pilgrimage site in France.

### ② Beuvron-en-Auge

One of the loveliest and most popular villages in the area. Charming houses, each one striped with old beams and dripping with geraniums **(above)**, cluster around the main square.

### ③ Manoir de Coupesarte

A short track off the D47 brings you to the most romantic of all the Auge manors. It is privately owned, but you can enter the adjoining farmyard to see the late 15th-century timbered house.

### ④ Vimoutiers

In the centre of Vimoutiers is a statue of Marie Harel, the woman credited with inventing Camembert in the sleepy village of that name *(see p114)*. The Musée du Camembert tells the story.

### ⑤ St-Pierre-sur-Dives

This market town huddles round its huge, sheltering church, all that is left of the rich Benedictine abbey that once stood here *(see p97)*. The monks originally constructed the town's venerable market hall *(see 76)*.

**Map of Pays d'Auge**

### 6 Château de Vendeuvre

This elegant 18th-century château **(above)** contains a museum of miniature furniture *(see p55)* and some delightful water gardens.

### 7 Clermont-en-Auge

Seek out St-Michel-de-Clermont, a charming chapel with a panorama of the Pays d'Auge and marshland beyond.

### 8 Château de Crèvecoeur-en-Auge

A rare chance to look inside a medieval lord's fortified, moated Auge manor. The former agricultural buildings house a museum of oil prospecting, connected with the Schlumberger Foundation.

### 9 Distillerie Busnel, Cormeilles

At this distillery, you can learn about the process of making the apple brandy Calvados – and, of course, you can sample the results.

### THE CIDER ROUTE

If you like cider, you can do no better than to follow the signposted Route du Cidre, linking the Pays d'Auge's principal cider-making villages – such as the delightful Cambremer, Bonnebosq and Beuvron-en-Auge – by way of pretty backroads. The route also passes about 20 local producers (recognizable by the sign "Cru de Cambremer"), who offer tours of their cellars and tastings. Pick up the leaflet "Tourist Routes" at any tourist office.

### 10 Château St-Germain-de-Livet

A visit to this enchanting château feels like entering a private world. Outside, there are turrets, towers, timbers and cleverly patterned brickwork **(below)**; inside, you can see oak furniture, Renaissance frescoes and creaking floorboards.

### NEED TO KNOW

**MAP E3–4, F3–4**

■ Office du Tourisme: 11 rue d'Alençon, Lisieux; 02 31 48 18 10

*Château St-Germain-de-Livet:* **MAP F4**. Jan–Mar & Nov–Dec: 2–5pm Sat & Sun; Apr–Jun & Sep–Oct: 11am–6pm Tue–Sun; Jul–Aug: 10am–7pm daily. Adm charge

*Château de Vendeuvre:* **MAP E4**. May–Sep: 11am–6pm daily. Adm charge

*Château de Crèvecoeur-en-Auge:* **MAP E4**. Apr–Jun & Sep: 11am–6pm daily; Jul–Aug: 11am–7pm daily; Oct: 2–6pm Sun. Adm charge

*Distillerie Busnel:* **MAP F3**. Cormeilles; 02 32 57 80 08.

Mar–mid-Nov: 10am–12:30pm & 2:30–7pm daily; mid-Nov–Dec: Sat & Sun. Adm charge

■ Beuvron-en-Auge makes a good lunch stop, with plenty of choice, including the gastronomic Pavé d'Auge *(see p74)*.

■ The sights listed here make an excellent circular driving tour.

# ⊞10 ⭐ Fondation Claude Monet, Giverny

Travelling by train between Vernon and Gasny in April 1883, Monet spotted Giverny through the window. It was love at first sight, and he moved here that year with Alice Hoschedé, who was later to become his wife. He planted his garden so that he could paint in every season. He considered it his masterpiece, a painting of dazzling colours created with nature. After his death, the house and garden fell into disrepair, but between 1977 and 1980 the Académie des Beaux-Arts restored them to their original condition – a living memorial to Monet and his work.

### 1 Water Garden
Exotic and asymmetrical, the water garden **(above)** is a place for calm contemplation of nature, among a riot of rhododendrons, willows, water lilies and more.

### 2 Water Lily Studio
His sight affected by cataracts, Monet built this large, light studio between 1914 and 1916, to work on his water lily series. It now houses the shop of the Fondation Claude Monet.

### 3 Japanese Bridge
This famous, wisteria-draped bridge **(above)** reflects Monet's abiding interest in Japanese prints, many of which are in the Pink House collection.

### 4 Clos Normand
Monet's French-style garden is a triumph of colour and judicious planting, with flowers in bloom all season.

### 5 Pink House
In this charming stucco house, Monet entertained Cézanne, Renoir, Matisse and other artists of the time.

### 6 Japanese Prints
Monet's precious woodblock prints are hung in several rooms around the house, according to a plan drawn up by the artist himself.

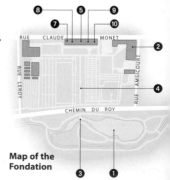

**Map of the Fondation**

### 7 Sitting-Room Studio
Monet used to retire to his simply furnished studio **(below)** after dinner to relax, smoke, and re-examine his day's work.

### 8 Dining Room
Imagine Monet, together with Alice Hoschedé, her children, and visiting artists and friends, seated around the large dining table in this perfectly restored room, painted in two shades of yellow, with faïence plates and Japanese prints on the walls, and vestiges of the dinner service in two dressers.

### 9 Monet's Bedroom
The room where Monet slept for 43 years, and eventually died, still has most of its original furniture, including a fine 18th-century inlaid desk. Endearingly, Monet kept works by the artists he most admired in his bedroom, among them Cézanne, Renoir, Manet, Pissarro and Rodin – a collection now scattered worldwide.

### 10 Kitchen
Little seems to have changed over the past century in this delightful room **(above)** – an extension built by Monet, with blue-and-white-tiled walls, a handsome cast-iron range, butler's sink, terracotta floor, and burnished copper pots and pans.

**NEED TO KNOW**

**MAP K4** ■ 84 rue Claude Monet, 27620 Giverny ■ 02 32 51 28 21 ■ www.fondation-monet.com

**Open** Apr–1 Nov: 9:30am–6pm daily

Adm: €9.50; students and children aged 7–12 €5.50, disabled €4, under-7s free

*Musée des Impressionnismes:* 99 rue Claude Monet, 27620 Giverny; 02 32 51 94 65; www.mdig.fr; Apr–mid-Nov: 10am–6pm daily. Adm: €7; ages 12–18 €4.50; ages 7–11 €3; under-7s free. Free first Sun of each month. Disabled access

■ For refreshments, try Hôtel Baudy (81 rue Claude Monet), or the café at the Musée des Impressionnismes.

■ Avoid the crowds by visiting early or late in the season.

**Sight Guide**
From the entrance on rue Claude Monet into an outbuilding, stairs lead down to the water lily studio. Outside is the Clos Normand. In the southwestern corner, an underground passage leads to the water garden and Japanese bridge. On entering the Pink House, beside the entrance, you must turn left and follow the circuit round from the small blue reading room to the sitting-room studio, then upstairs to the bedrooms. The tour ends with the dining room and kitchen.

# Musée des Impressionnismes, Giverny

**The vine-clad entrance to the museum**

## 1 The Museum
In the heart of the village of Giverny, the Musée d'Art Américain was replaced in 2009 by a museum entirely dedicated to the Impressionist movement exhibiting outstanding 19th- and 20th-century artworks. The Musée d'Orsay in Paris is its main partner.

## 2 The Collection
The museum features temporary exhibitions on the theme of Impressionism. There is a small permanent display showing Monet's influence on other artists.

## 3 Impressionist Painters
The artistic impact of the Impressionist movement on the second half of the 20th century is explored, with works by world-famous and lesser-known artists.

## 4 The Building
Terraced into the hillside, with vine-clad roofs, the building was designed by Philippe Robert to blend in with its surroundings. Inside, there are three large exhibition galleries and a 200-seat auditorium, used for conferences.

## 5 Exhibitions
The museum houses about two exhibitions each year, mostly showcasing works on loan from the Musée d'Orsay and from private collections.

## 6 Museum Gardens
In landscape architect Mark Rudkin's design, flowerbeds are planted simply in monochromatic colour schemes, divided by hedges. In 2006, the gardens were awarded Jardin Remarquable status.

## 7 The Terra Café
Enjoy quiches, salads, grilled fish, meat and American-style pies at this elegant café. There is also a tea room, and a pretty terrace in the heart of the garden.

## 8 The Hills of Giverny
At the back of the museum, a large meadow opens out onto a hill filled with poppies, daisies and cornflowers. This is the very landscape that inspired Monet. A walk through this meadow is a good way to immerse yourself in the Impressionist mindset.

## 9 Guided Tours
Informative audio tours and guided tours of the current exhibitions are available in English and other languages for both individuals and small groups.

**A guided tour of an exhibition**

## 10 Concerts and Events
www.mdig.fr
From April to October, concerts and other events are staged in the auditorium and garden. Check the website for more details.

## MONET AND IMPRESSIONISM

**Claude Monet**

As a child, Monet was encouraged to paint *en plein air* (outdoors). He subsequently found the established techniques of studio-painting inadequate for his purposes. Fascinated by the illusory effects of sunlight and the weather on his subjects, he strived to "capture the moment" with quick, bold brushstrokes, and was concerned more with effect than with sharp, naturalistic detail – a novel technique that did not endear him to the Salon despite his early success. His painting *Impression, Sunrise*, exhibited in a show with other sympathetic artists, led a critic to coin the term "Impressionism", and he was heralded as the father of the style.

Monet's discovery of Giverny coincided with a new energy and confidence in his painting. The colours in his carefully planned garden provided him with an ever-changing palette, and in the years he spent in Giverny, he painted his best-known works. Until then his life had been dogged by financial hardship and tragedy; at Giverny, he was solvent and successful for the first time.

### TOP 10 EVENTS IN MONET'S LIFE

**1** 1840: born on 14 November in Paris

**2** 1858: introduced to painting *en plein air* by Eugène Boudin

**3** 1866: enjoys first success at the Salon

**4** 1870: introduced to art dealer Paul Durand-Ruel

**5** 1871: starts collecting Japanese prints

**6** 1874: holds the first "Impressionist" exhibition with Renoir, Sisley and other artists

**7** 1883: discovers Giverny and moves into the Pink House

**8** 1892: starts work on the garden and Rouen Cathedral series; marries Alice Hoschedé

**9** 1916: starts his famous *Water Lily* series

**10** 1926: dies on 6 December at Giverny

*Water Lilies*, Claude Monet

# The Top 10 of Everything

Interior of Abbaye-aux-Hommes, Caen

# 🔟 Moments in History

**Gallic leader Vercingetorix surrendering to Julius Caesar**

### ① 58–51 BC: Roman Invasion

By 56 BC the Romans had swept through the region, conquering the Celtic Gallic settlers. They built roads, viaducts and fortified settlements, including Rotomagus (Rouen) and Augustodurum (Bayeux).

### ② 911: Treaty of St-Clair-sur-Epte

By the early 10th century, the Carolingian King Charles the Simple realized that the Vikings, who had invaded in 800, would not go quietly, so he ceded Rouen and the east of the region to them, making their leader Rollo the first duke of Normandy.

### ③ 1066: Norman Conquest

When Edward the Confessor died with no heir, his cousin William saw his chance to claim the English throne. He set sail on 27 September 1066, triumphed at Hastings on 14 October, and was crowned King of England on Christmas Day.

### ④ 1204: Union of Normandy and France

Since the accession of Henry II, King of England and Duke of Normandy, the French had tried to wrest control of the duchy from England. They succeeded in 1204, when King John lost Normandy to Philippe Auguste.

### ⑤ 1315: Normandy Charter

Signed by Louis X, this charter gave the region provincial autonomy, a sovereign court of justice in Rouen, and control over taxes. In return, local taxes were increased dramatically – amounting to a quarter of the country's tax bill.

### ⑥ 1450: French Recovery of Normandy

In the final phase of the Hundred Years' War, the decisive Battle of Formigny saw the French use guns and heavy cavalry to inflict a major defeat on English archers.

**The bloody Battle of Formigny**

The battle marked the end of fighting in Normandy and led to its recovery by France.

### 7 1789: Caen Revolt

During the French Revolution, there were royalist pockets throughout Normandy, but Caen became a centre for the republican Girondin movement (many of whose members originally came from the Gironde). Like the republicans who stormed the Bastille, their Norman counterparts demolished the château prison in Rouen.

### 8 1940: German Occupation

On 7 June 1940, the German army marched into Forges-les-Eaux and, two days later, into Rouen. This was the prelude to four years of occupation, during which many local people were imprisoned, tortured, deported and executed.

**German tanks in occupied Rouen**

### 9 1944: D-Day

In June 1944, Norman beaches became the target for Operation Overlord (see p37). By 20 August, Allied forces were advancing towards Paris over the Perche hills. Rouen was liberated on 30 August.

### 10 2014: 70th Anniversary of D-Day

Every 10 years, surviving D-Day veterans gather to commemorate the dead; the 2014 gathering will, for many, have been the last.

---

**TOP 10 HISTORIC CHARACTERS**

**Charles de Gaulle**

**1 Clovis**
Merovingian King Clovis (465–511) founded the French state by defeating the Romans and uniting the tribes.

**2 Rollo**
After signing the Treaty of St-Clair-sur-Epte, Viking leader Hrølf (c.854–928) was named Rollo, and became the first duke of Normandy.

**3 William Long Sword**
Rollo's acquisitive warrior son (c.893–943) extended the duchy's boundaries by taking Cotentin and southern Manche.

**4 William the Conqueror**
William (1027–87), the illegitimate son of Robert the Magnificent, united Normandy and conquered England.

**5 Matilda**
While abroad, William left Normandy in the capable hands of his wife Matilda (c.1031–83).

**6 Richard the Lionheart**
Richard (1157–99) became duke of Normandy in 1189. In 1196, he built Château Gaillard to protect Rouen.

**7 Joan of Arc**
A country girl, Joan (1412–31) was called by "angelic voices" to save France from English domination (see p27).

**8 Samuel de Champlain**
Explorer de Champlain (1567–1635) founded the city of Quebec.

**9 Charlotte Corday**
Educated in Caen, Girondin sympathizer Corday (1768–93) killed revolutionary Jean-Paul Marat in his bath.

**10 Charles de Gaulle**
Leader of the Free French, de Gaulle (1890–1970) came ashore at Juno Beach on 14 June 1944 to reclaim France from the Germans.

# 🔟 Artists in Normandy

*Mussel Collectors at Berneval,*
*Pierre-August Renoir*

## 1 Pierre-Auguste Renoir
Monet's great friend and fellow Impressionist Renoir (1841–1919) did not discover Normandy until he came to the coast in 1879, the year he painted *Mussel Collectors at Berneval*. He became a regular visitor to Giverny.

## 2 Claude Monet
The founder and leading light of Impressionism was brought up in Le Havre. Having moved to Paris, he returned regularly to paint in Honfleur, Rouen, Étretat and Varengeville. In 1883 he settled in Giverny, where he spent the rest of his life *(see pp40–43)*.

## 3 Jean-François Millet
Son of a peasant farmer in Gréville-Hague, Millet (1814–75) was apprenticed in Cherbourg before moving to Paris, where he worked under Paul Delaroche. He later moved to Barbizon, where he became a member of the Barbizon School led by Théodore Rousseau. He is best known for his gritty paintings of toiling farm workers.

## 4 Théodore Géricault
Born into a rich Rouen family, Géricault (1791–1824) shocked contemporaries with the realism and drama of paintings such as *The Raft of the Medusa*.

## 5 J M W Turner
The greatest English landscape artist of his time, Turner (1775–1851) paid frequent visits to Dieppe, Le Havre, Rouen and the Seine estuary. His vibrant watercolours had a profound influence on the young Monet.

*Étretat – A Windmill,* Jean-Baptiste Corot

### 6 Jean-Baptiste Corot

Corot (1796–1875) was a landscape artist who turned to portrait painting late in his career. The picturesque town of Étretat (see pp30–31) had particular appeal for him, and he travelled there with Courbet in the 1860s and 1870s.

### 7 Gustave Courbet

First of the French Realists, Courbet (1819–77) spent time in Trouville and accompanied Corot to Étretat. His stormy seascapes greatly influenced the Impressionists.

*People on the Beach at Trouville,* **Boudin**

### 8 Eugène Boudin

Brought up in Honfleur, Boudin (1824–98) did not have to go far to paint his seascapes. An advocate of painting in the open air – a practice he introduced to Monet – he was preoccupied with light and its effects on his subject matter. His loose brushstrokes heralded Impressionist techniques.

### 9 Georges Braque

Braque (1882–1963), who learned to paint while working for his decorator father in Le Havre, was attracted to the Fauve artists, but an encounter with Picasso transformed his style. In later years, he painted local landscapes and made stained glass in a studio in Varengeville.

### 10 Raoul Dufy

Only after flirtations with Impressionism and Fauvism did Dufy (1877–1953), a Le Havre native, find his own style. His subjects include carefree, ephemeral scenes, many in the coastal towns of Normandy.

---

**TOP 10 PAINTINGS OF NORMANDY**

*Water Lilies,* **Claude Monet**

**1 Rouen Cathedral Series (Monet)**
Painted between 1891 and 1895. One of the paintings is displayed in the Musée des Beaux-Arts, Rouen.

**2 Water Lily Series (Monet)**
Painted between 1899 and 1926. A number of these paintings are on show at the Musée de l'Orangerie, Paris.

**3 Impression: Sunrise (Monet)**
Painted in Le Havre in 1872. Displayed in the Musée Marmottan, Paris.

**4 The Gleaners (Millet)**
Painted in 1857. On show at the Musée d'Orsay, Paris.

**5 The Cliff at Étretat after the Storm (Courbet)**
Painted in 1869. Displayed in the Musée d'Orsay, Paris.

**6 Wheat-field in Normandy (Dufy)**
Painted in 1935. On show at the Musée Eugène Boudin, Honfleur.

**7 People on the Beach at Trouville (Boudin)**
Painted in 1865. Exhibited at the Musée Eugène Boudin, Honfleur.

**8 View from the Port of Dieppe (Pissarro)**
Painted in 1902. Displayed in the Château-Musée de Dieppe.

**9 The Fish Market, Honfleur (Dubourg)**
Painted in 1876. Displayed in the Musée Eugène Boudin, Honfleur.

**10 View of the Coast of Normandy (Richard Parkes Bonington)**
Painted in 1823. Exhibited at the Louvre, Paris.

# 🔟 Writers in Normandy

**Gustave Flaubert**

## 1 Gustave Flaubert

Flaubert spent the greater part of his 59 years in Normandy; its places and people suffuse his writing. Born in Rouen in 1821, he abandoned law training in Paris to live and write in Croisset until his death. He published his finest work, *Madame Bovary*, in 1857.

## 2 Guy de Maupassant

Maupassant (1850–93) was born at Château de Miromesnil near Dieppe, and spent his childhood in Étretat. His mother was a family friend of Flaubert, who would guide Maupassant's debut as a writer. His first masterpiece was *Boule de Suif*, published in 1880.

## 3 Marcel Proust

Proust was born in Paris in 1871 and died there in 1922. His *A la Recherche du Temps Perdu* is permeated by memories of Normandy – perhaps most notably the Grand Hôtel at Cabourg (*see p33*), which he renamed Balbec.

## 4 Pierre Corneille

The classical dramatist Pierre Corneille (1606–84) was born in Rouen. His plays *Le Cid*, *Horace*, *Cinna* and *Polyeucte* formed the yardstick for French tragedy. *Le Menteur* is, however, a comic masterpiece. His writing often reflects the tension between regional and national loyalties.

## 5 André Gide

Born in 1869 to a Huguenot father and Norman mother, Gide spent the early and latter parts of his life in Normandy. He saw the realities of life here, first as mayor of a commune, and later as a juror in Rouen. He won the Nobel Prize for Literature four years before his death in 1951.

## 6 Alain Chartier

Poet and political writer Alain Chartier (c.1390–c.1430) was best known for *La Belle Dame sans Merci* – a poem on courtly love. Born into a distinguished Bayeux family, he wrote his earliest-known poem, *Livre des Quatre Dames*, after France's defeat at the Battle of Agincourt in 1415.

**Jules Barbey d'Aurevilly**

## 7 Jules Barbey d'Aurevilly

Barbey (1808–89), novelist, commentator, conversationalist – and as an admirer of Byron and Brummell, inveterate dandy – was still able to scandalize at 66, when he published *Les Diaboliques*. Born in St-Saveur-le-Vicomte, he was raised on a diet of Norman tales told by a family servant.

## 8 Robert Wace

What little is known about the poet Robert Wace (c.1115–c.1183) comes from his last work, *Roman de Rou*, a verse history of the dukes of

Normandy. Educated in Caen, he wrote his romances for the great and good living around this area.

### 9 François Malherbe

The classical poet Malherbe (1555–1628) left Caen to study in Paris, Basle and Heidelberg. He worked for Henri d'Angoulême (*grand prieur* of France and governor of Provence) for 10 years before returning home. Called to Court in 1605, he became the strict arbiter of French literary style.

**François Malherbe**

### 10 Jacques Prévert

Prévert (1900–77) visited Normandy in 1930 and fell in love with it. Soon after, he started to write poetry on the themes of beauty, innocence, love and despair. *Paroles*, his best-known collection, was published in 1945. In 1971, he and his wife bought a house in Omonville-la-Petite. They are buried nearby, and there is a memorial garden in St-Germain-des-Vaux.

**Jacques Prévert**

## TOP 10 BOOKS SET IN NORMANDY

**Annie Ernaux**

**1 Madame Bovary (Gustave Flaubert)**
Set near the author's native Rouen, this classic ruffled contemporary feathers.

**2 A Day in the Country and Other Stories (Guy de Maupassant)**
Twenty-eight of Maupassant's brilliant short stories.

**3 The Secret Life of the Seine (Mort Rosenblum)**
The true story of a journey from Burgundy to Le Havre by houseboat.

**4 A Woman's Story (Annie Ernaux)**
A lovely tribute to the author's mother, who lived much of her life in Yvetot.

**5 The Bayeux Tapestry (Wolfgang Grape)**
The story of the Norman Conquest as told through the Bayeux Tapestry.

**6 Mont-St-Michel and Chartres (Henry Brooks Adams)**
A meditation on the medieval world, as seen through two of its most famous Gothic cathedrals.

**7 D-Day: The Battle for Normandy (Antony Beevor)**
A vivid and poignant account of the D-Day landings, packed with gripping biographical detail.

**8 Gardens in Normandy (Valery, Motte and Sarramon)**
A tour of forty spectacular gardens.

**9 Chantemesle: A Normandy Childhood (Robin Fedden)**
A lyrical account of an enchanted rural childhood in the region.

**10 A Normandy Tapestry (Alan Biggins)**
Biggins' account of his move to France with his family, which took him behind the scenes of French rural life.

# 🔟 Norman Abbeys

**Le Bec-Hellouin monastery**

### 1 Le Bec-Hellouin

In 1034, a knight called Herluin exchanged his charger for a donkey and founded a religious community on the banks of the River Risle. When he was joined some eight years later by the influential Italian theologians Lanfranc and Anselm, the monastery grew to become the intellectual heart of Normandy. Disbanded during the Revolution and later demolished, it again became a Benedictine monastery in 1948 *(see pp78 & 97)*.

### 2 Mont-St-Michel

Dramatically sited on a lone rock in the Bay of Mont-St-Michel, this famous medieval walled city is one of the most visited attractions in France *(see pp12–15)*.

### 3 Jumièges

A centre of learning for 700 years, monumental Jumièges became nothing more than a quarry after the Revolution. Today, its enigmatic ruins, romantically set in a loop of the Seine, live again as one of the top "must-see" sights of Normandy *(see pp22–3)*.

### 4 Abbaye-aux-Dames, Caen

**MAP D3**

Like their founders William and Matilda, the Abbaye-aux-Hommes and Abbaye-aux-Dames (the first of the two to be built) are close cousins. The imposing convent buildings, built to accommodate girls from the Norman aristocracy, were designed by Guillaume de la Tremblaye.

### 5 St-Wandrille

Founded in 649 and rebuilt in the 10th century after destruction by Vikings, the abbey became a centre of learning. Inevitably, the Revolution saw its demise, but in 1931 it became a Benedictine monastery again *(see p88)*.

### 6 La Trinité, Fécamp

This vast, beautiful church owes its scale to a casket containing the Holy Blood of Christ, said to have been washed ashore in the 1st century. The abbey, built on the spot in the 12th to 13th centuries, attracted streams of pilgrims. The relic, Le Précieux Sang, is still venerated today *(see p86)*.

**The striking Mont-St-Michel**

### 7 St-Georges, St-Martin-de-Boscherville

In 1114, William of Tancarville founded a small community of monks, who took this beautiful Norman Romanesque building as their abbey church *(see p88)*.

### 8 Abbaye-aux-Hommes, Caen

Lanfranc was the first abbot of the abbey, founded by William the Conqueror and consecrated in his presence in 1077. Ten years later, William was buried, most unceremoniously, in the abbey's church, St-Etienne *(see p97)*.

**Abbaye-aux-Hommes**

### 9 Hambye

Lord of the Manor Guillaume Paynel founded the abbey in 1145. Always a small community, its fortunes declined over the years, and in 1784 it was declared defunct. In the 19th century, the buildings were quarried for stone; only in the 20th century were the noble ruins visible today saved from further destruction *(see p104)*.

### 10 La Trappe
**MAP F5 ▪ Soligny-la-Trappe**

Founded in 1140, La Trappe was one of the Cistercian monasteries that adopted the Strict Observance – silence, prayer, abstinence, manual labour – introduced by the Abbot de Rancé in the 1660s. They were known thereafter as Trappist monasteries; there is another in the northwestern town of Briquebec.

**TOP 10 RELIGIOUS FIGURES**

Abbot de Rancé

**1 St Ouen**
Credited with reviving Christian zeal in the Rouen region. As a result, several abbeys were founded.

**2 St Philibert**
Gascon court favourite and protégé of St Ouen, Philibert founded Jumièges in the 7th century.

**3 St Wandrille**
Nobleman founder of the abbey in 649. Known as God's True Athlete for his remarkable physique.

**4 St Aubert**
Bishop of Avranches, to whom, legend has it, the Archangel Gabriel appeared in 708, ordering him to build a chapel on Mont-St-Michel.

**5 Lanfranc**
Influential Italian lawyer-monk (1005–1089). Became William the Conqueror's archbishop at Canterbury.

**6 St Anselm**
Philosopher-monk (1033–1109) who joined Lanfranc at Bec and succeeded him as archbishop of Canterbury.

**7 Joan of Arc**
Teenage soldier (1412–31) whose "voices" told her to save France from the English. She was captured and burned at the stake, but canonized in 1920.

**8 Guillaume de la Tremblaye**
Benedictine monk at Bec. A master architect and sculptor (1644–1715).

**9 Abbot de Rancé**
Nobleman who renounced his former life and founded the Trappists in 1664.

**10 St Thérèse Martin**
Deeply spiritual young nun (1873–97), whose shrine at Lisieux is venerated.

# 🔟 Museums and Galleries

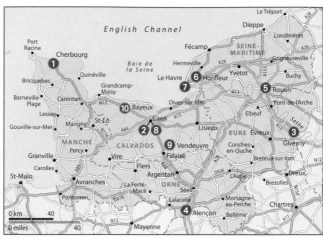

## 1 La Cité de la Mer, Cherbourg

MAP B2 ■ Gare Maritime Transatlantique, Cherbourg ■ Open Feb–mid-Mar, Apr–Jun & Sep: 9:30am–6pm daily; mid-Mar–end Mar: 10am–6pm; Jul–Aug: 9:30am–7pm; Oct–Dec: 10am–6pm. Closed Christmas to end Jan ■ Adm charge

This former maritime station is home to Europe's deepest aquarium. A superb *Titanic* exhibition includes mock-ups of the interior of the ill-fated ship. There's also a nuclear-powered submarine to explore. All of this introduces the visitor to the wonders of the underwater world, and to human adventures and achievements there.

**Marine life at La Cité de la Mer**

## 2 Le Mémorial de Caen

MAP D3 ■ Esplanade General Eisenhower ■ Open Feb–Oct: 8am–7pm daily; Nov–Dec: 9:30am–6pm daily ■ Adm charge

A moving and contemplative museum of remembrance, the Mémorial takes the visitor on a journey through the causes and consequences of World War II and the ensuing Cold War, using a host of interactive and audiovisual techniques, as well as fascinating archive footage. An extension to the museum is used as a place of reflection on peace.

## 3 Musée des Impressionnismes, Giverny

This museum is the only one in France that is wholly devoted to the influential Impressionist movement. It aims to explore the international nature of Impressionism (see p42).

## 4 Musee de Beaux-Arts et de la Dentelle, Alençon

MAP E6 ■ Cour Carrée de la Dentelle, Alençon ■ Open 10am–noon & 2–6pm Tue–Sun (Jul–Aug: daily) ■ Adm charge

In 1665, lacemakers in Alençon were given the challenge of creating lace equal in quality and popular appeal to that of Venice. They succeeded, coming up with a new and better technique, which made Alençon lace supreme until demand dropped in the 20th century. The story is told here, along with exquisite, intricate examples of the craft.

### 5 Musée des Beaux-Arts, Rouen

Monet's study of Rouen Cathedral and Corot's *Quayside Trade in Rouen* are among the highlights at this important art museum. Its collection is strong on old masters, as well as the Impressionists *(see p26)*.

### 6 Musée Eugène Boudin, Honfleur

Honfleur's rich artistic heritage is celebrated in this appealing museum, which includes works by Boudin himself, as well as by Monet *(see p20)*.

### 7 Musée Malraux, Le Havre

MAP E2 ▪ 2 bd Clemenceau, Le Havre ▪ Open 11am–6pm Wed–Fri & Mon, 11am–7pm Sat & Sun ▪ Adm charge

This innovative building, constructed from glass and metal, offers views of the port through a monumental concrete sculpture known as "The Eye", and is filled with light. The museum spans five centuries of art history and is home to the second largest collection of Impressionist paintings in France.

### 8 Musée des Beaux-Arts, Caen

MAP D3 ▪ Le Château ▪ Open Apr–Sep: 9:30am–6:30pm Wed–Mon; Oct–Mar: 9:30am–noon & 2–6pm Wed–Mon ▪ Adm charge

A superb collection of European paintings, dating from the 15th to the 20th centuries, is set in William the Conqueror's hilltop château. Perugino's *The Marriage of the Virgin* is a highlight.

### 9 Musée du Mobilier Miniature, Vendeuvre

This collection of 16th- to 19th-century miniature furniture is fascinating for its meticulous craftsmanship *(see p39)*.

**Musée du Mobilier Miniature display**

### 10 Bayeux Tapestry

Embroidered in 1077, this much-loved treasure recounts, with astonishing detail and drama, the story of Duke William's conquest of England. Galleries leading up to the tapestry bring the history vividly to life. The cloth itself – all 70 m (230 ft) of it – is behind glass *(see pp16–17)*.

**Detail from the famous 70-m- (230-ft-) long Bayeux Tapestry**

# TOP 10 Unspoiled Villages

**Granite houses lining the historic harbour at Barfleur**

### 1 Barfleur

The long tradition of fishing in Normandy is embodied in the charming port of Barfleur. Brightly painted fishing boats jostle in the harbour, overlooked by stern granite houses braced for all weathers. Beaches and a lighthouse you can visit add to the appeal *(see p107)*.

### 2 St-Fraimbault
**MAP D6**

St-Fraimbault is a true *village fleurie*. Each spring, 100,000 flowers swamp the village in colour as villagers try to outdo each other's displays. It all culminates in a mid-August festival.

### 3 Lyons-la-Forêt

A captivating medley of 16th- to 18th-century half-timbered buildings, Lyons-la-Forêt is set deep in the lovely Forêt de Lyons. It starred in both the 1934 Jean Renoir and the 1991 Claude Chabrol film versions of *Madame Bovary*, whose intangible influence still permeates the area *(see pp63 & 87)*.

### 4 Beuvron-en-Auge

All the charms of the Pays d'Auge are to be found in Beuvron-en-Auge. Its flower-decked houses are prettily striped and patterned with timber. On the south side of the central square, the delightful 15th-century Vieux Manoir is elaborately decorated with wood carvings *(see pp38 & 98)*.

### 5 Putot-en-Auge
**MAP E3**

This sleepy Pays d'Auge village has little more than a church (with a fine Romanesque portal and a cemetery for Allied soldiers), manor house and little brick-built *mairie* (town hall), but it somehow encapsulates the rural delights of the Auge region. Nearby Criqueville-en-Auge is also worth a visit for its enchanting 16th-century manor house.

### 6 Montville
**MAP G2**

At the confluence of two rivers – Clérette and Cailly – Montville is distinctive for flowers and fire engines. A *village fleurie*, it has an attractive lake, a park with a superb 300-year-old purple beech, and the Musée des Sapeurs-Pompiers (Museum of the

**Picturesque Lyons-la-Forêt**

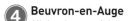

Fire Brigade). Full of old hand pumps and gleaming red fire engines, this fascinating museum traces the history of the French fire brigade from the early 18th century onwards.

## 7 Le Bec-Hellouin
### MAP G3

A quintessential Norman village set among fields and apple orchards, Le Bec-Hellouin takes its name from the stream that runs beside it and from the Norman knight Herluin, founder of the impressive 11th-century Benedictine abbey. Half-timbered houses and colourful window boxes add to the charm.

## 8 St-Valéry-en-Caux
### MAP G1

Encircled by high cliffs, this fishing village and child-friendly seaside resort occupies a charming spot on the Côte d'Albâtre, where tranquil Pays de Caux countryside meets beaches, boats and bikinis. The village is also home to the Maison Henri IV, a fine timber-framed Renaissance house on the quay.

## 9 Allouville-Bellefosse
### MAP G2

An extraordinary oak tree, thought to be at least 1,300 years old, has put this little village on the map. Inside the huge trunk are a sanctuary and a hermit's cell fashioned by a local priest in 1696. Nearby, in an old farmhouse deep in the countryside, is the Musée de la Nature, with displays dedicated to the local landscape, flora and fauna.

**Ancient oak at Allouville-Bellefosse**

## 10 St-Céneri-le-Gérei

This enchanting village has a memorable setting. Crowned by a fine Romanesque church, its stone houses overlook the gentle River Sarthe as it flows around a rocky promontory on the edge of the Alpes Mancelles (see p114).

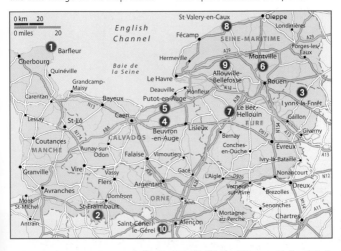

*Following pages* Half-timbered houses at Le Bec-Hellouin

# 🔟 Areas of Natural Beauty

**River in La Suisse Normande**

## 1 La Suisse Normande

Centred around the River Orne, this region of gentle hills, rocky cliffs, woods and charming villages is hardly reminiscent of Switzerland, but still attracts its share of hikers and tourists. Well placed for exploring, the capital Clécy is also a centre for climbing, canoeing and hang-gliding (see p95).

## 2 Pays d'Auge

When most people think of Normandy, they picture apple orchards, manor houses, rolling meadows dotted with cows, and timbered farmhouses. This is the Pays d'Auge (see pp38–9), the rural hinterland to the Côte Fleurie, and home to cider, Calvados and some of France's best-known cheeses, including Camembert. It is also home to the Basilique Ste Thérèse de Lisieux, a long tradition of horse breeding, and *teurgoule* – a rice pudding.

## 3 Parc Naturel Régional de Normandie-Maine

Normandy's largest regional park spans 2,350 sq km (900 sq miles) of Basse-Normandie and Pays de la Loire, with scenery that ranges from deep forests to gently rolling hills, and from marshland to meadows. The park aims to preserve rural traditions by promoting local arts and crafts, agriculture, forestry and outdoor activities (see p112).

## 4 Parc Naturel Régional des Boucles de la Seine Normande

MAP G2 ■ Maison du Parc: Notre-Dame-de-Bliquetuit ■ 02 35 37 23 16

Following the snaking loops (boucles) of the Seine, this 580-sq-km (224-sq-mile) park between Rouen and Le Havre was originally known as the Parc Naturel Régional de Brotonne. It embraces forests (notably the Brotonne), pastures and the Marais Vernier wetlands. It is also the starting point for the Route des Fruits, a picturesque 30-km (19-mile) cycle route through apple, pear, cherry and plum orchards.

## 5 Pays d'Ouche

MAP F5

As you journey from north to south, the landscape changes from the heavily wooded Eure to the lush green countryside of the Orne. Spanning both, the Pays d'Ouche is blessed with abundant streams, rivers and lakes, making it a paradise for anglers.

## 6 Pays de Caux

MAP G1–2, H1–2

Extending south from the striking white cliffs of the Côte d'Albâtre,

**Côte d'Albâtre, Pays de Caux**

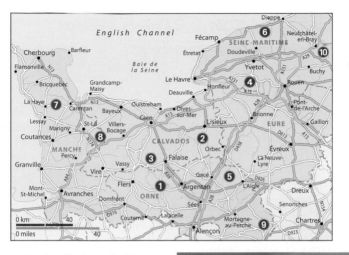

and bordered by the fertile Seine and Bresle valleys, this immense chalky plateau provides wonderfully rich soil for arable farmland. You can catch glimpses of the farmsteads' half-timbered buildings and apple orchards through their massive stone gateways.

### 7 Parc Naturel Régional des Marais du Cotentin et du Bessin

MAP B3 ■ Maison du Parc: Les Ponts d'Ouve, St Côme du Mont ■ 02 33 71 65 30

The wetlands that characterize this park stretch 1,250 sq km (480 sq miles) from Les Veys to Lessay. The eastern marshes are home to many species of migrating birds and small mammals, which can be observed and studied from the park's hides and nature reserves.

### 8 Pays de Bocage
MAP C4

From the south of Cotentin down to southwest Calvados, this is an intensely rural and unspoiled stretch of countryside, much loved by ramblers – a patchwork of meadows, interrupted only by woods, rivers, picturesque villages and the distinctive network of hedgerows that gives the region its name.

Parc Naturel Régional du Perche

### 9 Parc Naturel Régional du Perche

MAP G6 ■ For information: Manoir de Courboyer, Noce ■ 02 33 25 70 10

Between the Beauce plains and the Pays de Bocage, this 1,820-sq-km (700-sq-mile) park was created in 1998. The high ground is forested and the lower slopes are planted with orchards and hedges. Châteaux and manor houses pepper the landscape.

### 10 Pays de Bray
MAP H2

Occupying land in the northeast formed by a geological fault known as the *boutonnière* (buttonhole), Normandy's least populated area contains the Béthune, Andelle and Epte rivers, and rich dairy pastures.

# 🔟 Forests

**Reflections in the Étang de la Herse, Forêt de Belleme**

## 1 Forêt de Belleme
MAP F6

This forest is dotted with large pools, including the lovely Étang de la Herse. Of its many splendid oak trees, the most famous is the Chêne de l'École on the western fringes – 40 m (130 ft) tall and more than 300 years old.

## 2 Forêt de Réno-Valdieu
MAP F6 & G6

Walk or cycle the path carved through the forest, and admire a magnificent line of giant oaks that soar up to 40 m (130 ft). They were planted in the 17th century, along with beech trees, to make planks for naval ships.

## 3 Forêt d'Eawy
MAP H2

Although the name Eawy (pronounced "Ee-a-vee") means wet pasture, this is a glorious beech forest covering 72 sq km (28 sq miles) on a jagged outcrop. It was originally planted with oaks, which were cut down to build houses after the Hundred Years' War. To see other species, follow the Chemin des Écoliers.

**The breathtaking Forêt d'Écouves**

## 4 Forêt d'Écouves
MAP E6

With its dense thickets of oak, beech, imported spruce and Scots pine, this is, at 140 sq km (54 sq miles), the region's largest and most beautiful forest. Its rich wildlife includes rare birds, deer and boar. The forest is also home to a 12th-century chapel, located in La Lande-de-Goult, which is known for its carved capitals.

### 5 Forêt de Brotonne
MAP G2

The heart of the Parc Naturel Régional des Boucles de la Seine Normande, this forest of towering oak, beech and pine, almost encircled by a loop in the Seine and reached by the soaring Brotonne Bridge, affords breathtaking views. It is home to deer, boar and hare, and in spring produces a carpet of bluebells.

### 6 Forêt d'Eu
MAP H1

This forest of beeches and many more exotic trees covers three large plateaux: Triage Forêt d'Eu, Haute Forêt d'Eu and Basse Forêt d'Eu. Among the highlights are a stunning view of the Yères Valley from Poteau de Ste-Cathérine, and a pair of intertwined oak and beech trees, known as the *bonne entente* (happy couple).

### 7 Forêt du Perche et de la Trappe
MAP F5

Glimpse the characteristic *étangs* (pools) through the trees from the D603, which bisects these two forests, usually regarded as one. A ramble here might turn into a mushroom hunt: the ferny floor is a breeding ground for ceps and chanterelles. Don't miss Abbaye de la Trappe *(see p53)*, home to Trappist monks.

### 8 Forêt de Roumare
MAP G3

With the Forêts de Rouvray, Verte and La Londe, Roumare forms a 140-sq-km (50-sq-mile) crown around Rouen. Roe and fallow deer and wild boar can be seen in the Parc Animalier (wildlife park) near Canteleu on its eastern border, where there is also a 15th-century subterranean convent in the caves of Ste-Barbe.

### 9 Forêt de Lyons
MAP H3 & J3

This 100-sq-km (37-sq-mile) forest was a favourite hunting ground of Merovingian kings. Tall beech trees cast a beautiful, dappled light, making

**Abbaye de Mortemer, Forêt de Lyons**

it a great place for walking. As well as Lyons-la-Forêt *(see p56 & p87)*, there are two châteaux and the ruined Abbaye de Mortemer to explore.

### 10 Forêt des Andaines
MAP D5

You might glimpse deer roaming through the forest that encircles Bagnoles-de-l'Orne, and you will certainly see different species of tree, including Japanese larch and Canadian fir. Try to visit the priory dedicated to St Ortaire, and the attractive observation tower of Bonvouloir.

**Bonvouloir tower, Forêt des Andaines**

# TOP 10 Parks and Gardens

## 1 Château de Canon
MAP E4 ■ Mézidon-Canon
■ Open May–Jun & Sep: 2–7pm
Wed–Mon; Jul & Aug: 11am–
1pm & 2–7pm daily ■ Adm charge

The highlights of this 18th-century Anglo-French park, with its pretty, Italianate château, are the Chartreuses, a series of walled gardens brimming over with flowers. Statues, a lake, a temple and a Chinese pavilion add further interest.

**Swans, Château de Canon**

## 2 Château de Vandrimare
MAP H3 ■ Vandrimare ■ Open
mid-Apr–Jul & Sep–mid-Oct: 2:30–
6pm Sat & Sun ■ Closed first weekend
every month and Aug ■ Adm charge

Each of these contemporary gardens is devoted to one of the five senses – sight, smell, sound, touch and taste. Set in a First Empire park, they include a maze, an orangery and over 2,500 plant species.

## 3 Jardins de Bellevue
MAP H2 ■ Beaumont-le-
Hareng ■ 02 35 33 31 37 ■ Open
10am–6pm daily ■ Adm charge

Two national flower collections – of *Meconopsis* (Himalayan blue poppy) and *Helleborus Orientalis* (Lenten rose) – are included in these lovely year-round gardens facing the Forêt d'Eawy (see p62).

## 4 Parc Zoologique Jean-Delacour
MAP G2 ■ Clères ■ 02 35 33 23 08
■ Open Apr–Sep: 10am–7pm daily;
Oct: 10am–noon & 1:30–6:30pm daily
■ Adm charge

This landscaped park surrounds the Renaissance château at Clères. Created in 1920 by naturalist Jean Delacour, the garden is populated with flamingos and exotic ducks, while in the park, animals such as kangaroos and gibbons roam.

## 5 Jardins Agapanthe
MAP H2 ■ Grigneuseville
■ Open Apr & Oct: 2–6pm
Sat & Sun; May–Sep: 2–7pm
Thu–Tue ■ Adm charge

Winding paths lead through lush foliage, over bridges, up and down steps, and through a pergola. There is an elegant mix of exotic species, topiary and flowers.

### 6 Jardin des Plantes, Rouen

MAP G3 ■ 114 av Martyrs de la Résistance ■ Open 8:30am–dusk daily

These tranquil public gardens in the heart of the city house a large and important botanical collection, including formal flowerbeds, rare trees, hothouses, an orangery, a rose garden, a rockery, and a collection of medicinal plants.

Orchid, Jardin des Plantes, Rouen

acid-loving plants such as rhododendrons and azaleas. Artists Cocteau, Monet and Braque were frequent visitors in their day.

### 8 Jardin d'Elle

MAP C4 ■ Villiers-Fossard ■ Open Mar–Nov: 9am–noon & 2–6pm Tue–Sat, 2–6pm Mon & Sun ■ Adm charge

With a maze of individually themed areas, this modern landscaped garden has more than 2,500 varieties of plants and trees.

### 9 Le Jardin Plume

MAP H3 ■ Auzouville sur Ry ■ 02 35 23 00 01 ■ Open mid-May–Oct: Wed–Sun (times vary; phone to check) ■ Adm charge

This contemporary garden in a typical Normandy orchard contrasts formal, geometrically patterned *parterres* with swathes of tall grasses and flowerbeds overflowing with asters and Japanese anemones.

### 10 Château de Brécy

MAP D3 ■ St-Gabriel-Brécy ■ Open Easter–Nov: 2:30–6:30pm Tue, Thu & Sun (Sat in Jun) ■ Adm charge

Five terraces of formal gardens sweep gracefully from the château towards the focal point: an ornate wrought-iron gate bearing the initials of Brécy's 17th-century owners. The gardens are thought to have been designed by François Mansart.

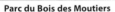

**Parc du Bois des Moutiers**

### 7 Parc du Bois des Moutiers

MAP G1 ■ Varengeville-sur-Mer ■ Open mid-Mar–mid-Nov: 10am–8pm daily ■ Adm charge

Edwin Lutyens and Gertrude Jekyll created the park and gardens for Guillaume Mallet, for whom Lutyens also built the house in 1898. Between here and the sea, the *valleuse* (dry valley) is filled with

**Aerial view of Château de Brécy**

# 🔟 Spas and Resorts

## 1 Forges-les-Eaux
### MAP H2

Quiet and dignified, Forges-les-Eaux became a fashionable spa town after it was visited in 1633 by a regal threesome: Louis XIII, his queen Anne of Austria, and Cardinal Richelieu. Today, the spa and casino, built in the 1950s, are run as a health and leisure complex.

**Windswept, sandy Barneville-Plage**

## 2 Barneville-Plage

Spectacular sandy beaches, backed by windblown dunes, sweep along the west coast of the Cotentin Peninsula, looking out towards the Channel Islands. At Barneville-Plage, between Barneville-Carteret and Portbail, the coast becomes tame enough for a holiday beach, full to bursting in summer, and backed by lines of villas (see p106).

## 3 Courseulles-sur-Mer
### MAP D3

Along the Côte de Nacre at Juno Beach, where memories of the Normandy invasion (see pp34–7) mingle with modern-day seaside amusements, Courseulles has a large marina – although it is somewhat overshadowed by modern apartment blocks. The tourist office runs guided tours on the D-Day landings on foot, by bike and in sand yachts.

## 4 Bagnoles-de-l'Orne

Legend has it that medieval lord Hugues de Tessé left his horse Rapide to die quietly of old age in the forest, only for the animal to trot home in rude health. He found that a spring was the cause of the miraculous recovery, bathed there himself, and was also rejuvenated. Today, this calm, orderly spa town attracts thousands to its Établissement Thermal, particularly helpful for rheumatism and circulatory problems (see p112).

## 5 Deauville and La Côte Fleurie

The magnificent coastline from Honfleur to Cabourg, with its series of wide, sandy beaches, means that all its resorts – Villerville, Trouville, Deauville, Villers-sur-Mer, Houlgate

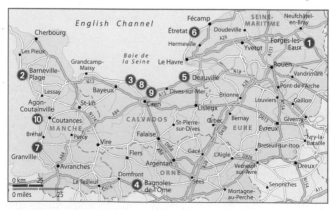

and Cabourg – have much to offer the sun-worshipper, with swimming and water sports all the way along. And if you tire of the beach, there are plenty of casinos where you can spend your money. Each place has its own character, none more so than exclusive Deauville *(see pp32–3)*.

**Curving bay at Étretat**

### 6 Étretat

With its shingle beach and esplanade curving between two famous chalk headlands (the Falaises d'Aval and d'Amont), its dramatic clifftop walks and its recreational Parc de Loisirs des Roches, charming and elegant Étretat is the Côte d'Albâtre's most alluring resort. Many writers and artists flocked here in the 19th century *(see pp30–31 & 86)*.

### 7 Granville

With its stern granite upper town on the one hand, and its beach and seaside amusements on the other, Granville has two quite different faces. It became fashionable as a resort in the 19th century. Among its current attractions, it boasts a thalassotherapy centre, the Aquarium du Roc (a "shell wonderland") and a lively casino *(see p105)*.

### 8 Luc-sur-Mer
MAP D3

Thalassotherapy (seawater treatment) is a speciality of Norman resorts, and at bracing Luc-sur-Mer, the cure uses kelp extract. There's also a seawater hammam. Children can fish for crabs, shrimps and clams from the shore, and admire the skeleton of a 19 m (76 ft) beached whale in the attractive municipal park.

### 9 Riva-Bella
MAP E3

The people of Caen, on the River Orne, are proud of their close connection to the sea, and here, at the mouth of the river, is "Caen-sur-Mer": the attractive ferry and yachting port of Ouistreham and the bustling resort of Riva-Bella, with its superb sandy beach and jolly main street, rue de la Mer.

### 10 Agon-Coutainville
MAP B4

With 8 km (5 miles) of fine, sandy beach, this west coast resort makes a great summer playground for the inhabitants of nearby Coutances and visitors alike. Spend a morning on the beach and then take an afternoon walk out to Pointe d'Agon, with its magnificent sea views.

**Granville's upper town and harbour**

# 🔟 Activities for Children

### 1 Parc Zoologique Cerzä
MAP F4 ▪ Hermival-les-Vaux
▪ 02 31 62 15 76 ▪ Open Feb–Mar &
Oct–Nov: 10am–5:30pm daily;
Apr–Jun & Sep: 9:30am–6:30pm
daily; Jul–Aug: 9:30am–7pm daily
▪ www.cerza.com ▪ Adm charge

To call Cerzä a zoo is to do it a
disservice. More than 50 hectares
(123 acres) have been set aside to
provide a natural environment for
African and endangered species,
including tigers and lemurs. It also
oversees breeding programmes.

**Giraffes, Parc Zoologique Cerzä**

### 2 Vélo Rail Experience
MAP D4–5 ▪ Between Caen
and Flers ▪ 02 31 69 39 30 ▪ www.
rails-collinesnormandes.fr ▪ Open
Apr–Oct ▪ Adm charge

Ride a pedal-powered "bicycle train"
and take in the spectacular scenery
along the disused railway lines in the
Orne and Noireau river valleys.

### 3 Parc de Loisirs L'Ange Michel
MAP C6 ▪ St-Martin-de-Landelles
▪ 02 33 49 04 74 ▪ Open mid-Apr–
May & Sep: 11am–6pm Sat & Sun,
public hols; Jun–mid-Jul: 10:30am–
6pm daily; mid-Jul–Aug: 10:30am–
7pm daily ▪ Adm charge

Electric go-karts, "Aqua-splash"
(boats that whizz down slides), dry-
slope sledges and plenty more keep
the children happy for hours here.

### 4 Étretat Aventure
MAP F2 ▪ Les Loges ▪ 02 35 29
84 45 ▪ Open Jul–Aug 1–8pm daily
(times vary the rest of the year) ▪ www.
etretat-aventure.fr ▪ Adm charge

In a lovely forest near Étretat, this
treetop rope park has five exciting
courses of varying difficulty – some
suitable for children as young as 3 –
high up among the trees. There are
also zip wires and a bungee jump.

### 5 Village Enchanté
MAP C5 ▪ Bellefontaine
▪ 07 61 13 40 64 ▪ Open Jul–Aug:
10:30am–6:30pm daily; May–Jun:
10:30am–6:30pm Sat & Sun ▪ www.
village-enchante.fr ▪ Adm charge

A stunning park forms the setting
for this fantasy village. Enchanted
trails, bouncy castles and pony rides
are aimed at the under-12s, with
go-karts and zip wires for older kids.

### 6 Alligator Bay
MAP B5 ▪ Beauvoir ▪ 02 33 68
11 18 ▪ Open Feb–Mar & Oct–Nov:
2–6pm daily; Apr–Sep: 10am–7pm
daily ▪ Adm charge

Meet alligators, crocodiles, lizards
and tortoises at this wildlife park.

### 7 Musée du Chemin de Fer Miniature
MAP D4 ▪ Clécy ▪ Open mid-Apr–
early Jul: 2–6pm Mon & Fri, 10am–
noon & 2–6pm Tue–Thu, Sat & Sun;
early Jul–Aug: 10am–6pm daily;
Sep: 2–5pm daily ▪ Adm charge

Visitors can admire one of Europe's
largest model railways, and then take
a miniature train ride around the site.

**Musée du Chemin de Fer Miniature**

Roller coaster ride at Festyland

### 8 Festyland
MAP D3 ■ Caen-Carpiquet
■ 02 31 75 04 04 ■ Open Apr–Jun &
French school holidays: 11am–6pm
Wed, Sat, Sun & national holidays;
Jul–Aug: 10:30am–7pm daily; Sep:
10:30am–6pm Sat & Sun ■ Adm charge

With a roller coaster and other
vertiginous rides, bouncy castles, water
slides and a 3-D cinema, this amuse-
ment park is for children of all ages.

### 9 Ludiver, Cap de la Hague
MAP A2 ■ Flottemanville-
Hague ■ Open Feb–Jun & Sep–Dec:
2–6pm Mon–Fri & Sun; Jul–Aug:
11am–6:30pm daily ■ Adm charge

A fascinating day out for young
scientists, Ludiver comprises
an observatory, planetarium and
meteorology station. Among
the treats on offer are a 3-D trek
through the solar system, a journey
to the centre of the Earth, and a
chance to view images from the
main (600mm) telescope, either
directly or in an indoor amphitheatre.

### 10 Artmazia
MAP H2 ■ Massy ■ 02 35 93 17
12 ■ Open Jul–Aug: 2:30–6:30pm
daily; May–Jun: 2:30–6:30pm Sat &
Sun; some eves in Aug ■ Adm charge

Find your way through the world's
longest maze, made up of 5,000
beech and hornbeam trees. The park
also has orchards and an art garden.

### TOP 10 TIPS FOR FAMILIES

**1 Restaurants**
Most places in Normandy are
child-friendly, can provide high chairs,
and offer an inexpensive *menu d'enfants*.

**2 Picnics**
A fun way to feed the family without
having to worry about the mess. Pack
picnic equipment and enjoy shopping
for food at local markets.

**3 Hotels**
In most hotels, children under 12
can sleep in a bed in their parents'
room at little or no extra cost.

**4 Gîtes**
For more space and flexibility, consider
renting a house or apartment (see p127).

**5 Car Travel**
If you're renting a car, book child
seats in advance. Stock up with water,
food and games before journeys.

**6 Trains**
Under-4s travel free on French
trains, as long as they sit on an adult's
knee; 4- to 12-year-olds can usually
travel for half the adult price.

**7 Tourist Trains**
A painless way to see the sights, these
trains run through various town centres.
Details are available from tourist offices.

**8 River Trips**
Organized trips with unique views of
the countryside include those on the
Douve and Taute in Cotentin (see p125).

**9 Farms**
Pet the animals and see country life
at close quarters at farms throughout
Normandy. Check with tourist offices.

**10 Sightseeing**
Children under 6 can visit many sights
for free; tickets for under-12s are
usually offered at a reduced price.

Feeding goats on a farm

# 🔟 Outdoor Activities

### ① Golf

Golfers are spoiled for choice in Normandy, which has 37 courses, 23 of them with 18 holes or more. Notable courses include Golf d'Étretat, situated on the clifftop above the famous Falaise d'Aval *(see p30)*, and Golf de Saint-Saëns, with beautiful views over the Forêt d'Eawy *(see p62)*. Deauville has no fewer than three top courses and there are fine courses at Omaha Beach and Granville.

**Horse riding through the countryside**

### ② Bases de Loisirs

Normandy has many *base de loisirs* (leisure bases) by lakes and on rivers, where you can enjoy swimming and water sports. Many also offer tennis, golf, riding, archery and other facilities.

### ③ Sand Yachting and Water Sports

Normandy's broad, sandy beaches lend themselves perfectly to sand yachting *(char à voile)*, particularly at Omaha Beach and along the west coast of the Cotentin Peninsula (there are large centres at Vauville and Portbail). You will also find windsurfing and kite-surfing on offer. Sailors can choose from around 100 sailing schools and clubs dotted along the coastline.

### ④ Horse Riding

Normandy has many equestrian centres – especially in the Orne, where, for example, Le Village du Cheval in St-Michel-des-Andaines offers a wide variety of horse-related activities. You can embark on a full-blown trekking holiday or just organize a few hours' riding through the countryside *(see p125)*.

### ⑤ Canoeing

Condé-sur-Vire is Normandy's largest canoeing and kayaking resort; the Vire valley makes a perfect family outing *(see pp104–5)*. Canoeing is also on offer at Pont d'Ouilly in the Suisse Normande, on the Eure near Pacy-sur-Eure, and at Saint-Saëns in the Pays de Bray.

### ⑥ Mountain Biking

The Perche is particularly suited to mountain biking, with marked trails at various levels of difficulty (maps are available from Mortagne-au-Perche and Domfront tourist offices). The terrain is also suitable in the Suisse Normande and at Amayé-sur-l'Orne.

### ⑦ Walking and Rambling

Normandy is wonderful walking country. Official footpaths (marked by red-and-white posts) crisscross the region, while the National Hiking Trails (Grandes Randonnées, or GR) provide spectacular long-distance routes. In Normandy, these include the

**Catamarans for rent on a beach**

GR23 (Seine and Forêt de Brotonne), GR223 (Cotentin Peninsula coast), and GR221 (Suisse Normande).

### 8 Fishing
The diversity of Norman lakes and rivers makes freshwater fishing a popular pastime. Sea-fishing expeditions are organized from ports including Honfleur, Trouville, Dieppe and St-Valéry-en-Caux.

### 9 Bungee Jumping
**MAP C4 ▪ AJ Hackett Bungy: 02 31 66 31 66 (reservations required)**
At the now defunct Souleuvre viaduct (built in 1889 by Gustave Eiffel), adrenaline junkies dive towards the ground secured by an elastic rope around the ankles, or scoot across the valley at 100 kph (60 mph) in a harness suspended from a cable.

**Bungee jumping at Souleuvre**

### 10 Cycling
Cycling is a great way to take in the Norman countryside. Each *département* has marked routes, with accompanying booklets available at tourist offices. In Manche, old railway lines and towpaths have been turned into cycle paths, while the forests of Lyons and Brotonne and the Eure and Seine valleys are excellent for cycling areas. The Veloscenic (www.veloscenic.com) route runs all the way from Paris to Mont-St-Michel.

**TOP 10 WALKS**

**Hiking, La Hague Peninsula**

**1 La Hague Peninsula**
The coastal path GR223 passes rugged countryside and the dramatic Nez de Jobourg (see pp103 & 107).

**2 Val de Saire**
This pastoral valley is a great place for a gentle country walk. Finish at St-Vaast-la-Hougue or at Barfleur (see pp106–7).

**3 Dunes and marshes, Bréhal**
MAP B4
Take the *route submersible* to see one of Cotentin's unique natural havens, Havre de la Vanlée – but be warned, the road becomes heavily flooded during the dramatic spring tides.

**4 Waterfalls of Mortain**
MAP C5
Follow the River Cance through the surrounding Alpine landscape.

**5 La Suisse Normande**
Rugged walking country, with great views from the Roche d'Oëtre (see p95).

**6 Pays d'Auge**
Rolling pastures, pretty villages, and plenty of stops for cheese and cider tastings (see pp38–9).

**7 Forêt du Perche et de la Trappe**
Combine walking with mushrooming amid woods and pools (see p63).

**8 L'Aigle**
Market day (Tue) is the best day for a walking tour of this historic town and its neighbouring cantons (see p114).

**9 Forêt d'Eawy**
Explore one of Normandy's most beautiful beech forests by walking the Chemin des Écoliers (see p62).

**10 The Seine**
Follow the GR23 along the Seine's south bank and into the beautiful Forêt de Brotonne (see p63).

# 🔟 Culinary Highlights

**Mère Poulard kitchen, Mont-St-Michel**

### 1 Omelette de la Mère Poulard

Annette Poulard (1861–1931) was the *patronne* of a Mont-St-Michel hotel. The exact recipe for her famously perfect omelettes, available at any time to hungry visitors who crossed the bay on foot or by horse and cart, is not known. We do know that she never let the butter brown, beat her eggs vigorously in a copper bowl (possibly separating yolks and whites first), and stirred continuously as she cooked them in her long-handled pan.

**Delicious *filets de sole Normande***

### 2 Poulet Vallée d'Auge

The key Norman ingredients, cider and cream, are combined to make this delicious chicken dish from the Pays d'Auge. Chicken pieces and mushrooms are sautéed in butter, then braised in a sauce of cider, Calvados and cream. Other traditional Norman dishes served in a sauce of cider and cream include *côtes de veau* (veal cutlets) and *filet de porc* (pork fillet).

### 3 Filets de Sole Normande

Occupying pride of place among the catch brought back by Normandy's fishermen is the magnificent Dover sole, in French, *sole Normande*. It is equally delicious cooked simply *à la meunière* (with butter), or, as in Dieppe, with shrimps and mussels in a creamy *velouté* sauce – and can be prepared in countless other ways.

### 4 Teurgoule

An enormously popular dessert, both in the home and in restaurants, this regional speciality dates back to the days when spices, brought to Honfleur and Dieppe by merchant ships from the East, first became popular. Local housewives discovered that a flavouring of cinnamon was the perfect partner for pudding rice baked with cream, and the recipe for *teurgoule* was born.

### 5 Marmite Dieppoise

This hearty fish stew was originally concocted in Dieppe as a way of using up the many different types of fish, shrimps and mussels. It is lightly flavoured with spices.

**6 Canard à la Rouennaise**

Tasting much better than it sounds, *canard à la Rouennaise* refers to ducklings that have been dispatched by smothering; as a result, the blood is prevented from escaping, giving a strong flavour to the meat. Traditionally, the bird is stuffed, then served in a sauce made of its own liver and blood.

**7 Tripes à la mode de Caen**

A popular country dish in Normandy; tripe from the local cattle is cooked simply *à la mode de Caen* with onions, calf's feet, Calvados and cider, while in Ferté-Macé it is made into little bundles *en brochette* (on skewers).

**8 Caille aux Monstrueux**

There are many ways to cook this Elbeuf speciality made with quail and leeks. The variety of leek cultivated in the Seine and Eure valleys is known as *monstrueux* ("monstrous" – they are short and fat), and its distinctive flavour perfectly complements the quail.

**9 Trou Normand**

This famous Norman indulgence refers to a shot of chilled Calvados thrown back between courses to aid digestion. The word *trou* means "hole": the shot of *calva* is said to create a hole for more food.

**10 Douillons and Bourdelots**

Most often found in cake shops rather than in restaurants, these individual, melt-in-the-mouth pastries are filled with a whole small apple or pear, peeled and cored and flavoured with cinnamon.

**A freshly baked apple *bourdelot***

**A selection of Normandy cheeses**

## TOP 10 CHEESES

**1 Camembert**
This world-famous cheese was invented by Marie Harel during the Revolution. By the 1880s, equipped with its famous box and label, it was being exported all over Europe.

**2 Livarot**
Another cheese with a long history, it tastes a great deal better than it smells.

**3 Neufchâtel**
Dating back to the 10th century, this creamy cheese comes as a heart, or in one of five other shapes.

**4 Pont l'Evêque**
Originally called Angelot, this square, washed rind cheese, matured in wooden boxes, has a long history and dates back to the Middle Ages.

**5 Pavé d'Auge**
This square, spicy cheese from the northern Pays d'Auge was a forerunner of Pont l'Evêque.

**6 Brillat-Savarin**
A triple-cream cheese invented by cheese-maker Henri Androuët.

**7 Fin-de-siècle**
Despite its name, the history of this triple-cream cheese, promoted by Androuët, is unknown.

**8 Fromage de Monsieur**
A strong cheese invented near Rouen and sold by a man whose name really was M Fromage (Mr Cheese).

**9 Coutances**
Packaged in a round box, this rich, creamy cheese has a thin crust.

**10 Briquebec**
This mild cheese was invented in the 19th century by the Trappist monks of the Abbaye de Briquebec in the *département* of Manche.

# TOP 10 Gourmet Restaurants

The elegant dining room at Manoir du Lys

### 1 Manoir du Lys, Bagnoles-de-l'Orne

MAP D5 ▪ La Croix Gauthier, rte de Juvigny-sous-Andaine ▪ 02 33 37 80 69 ▪ Closed Sun dinner, Mon & Tue lunch (mid-Feb–Apr & Nov–early Jan); Mon all day, Tue & Wed lunch (May–Oct) ▪ €€

Franck Quinton's cooking is rooted in local tradition but also respects contemporary trends. He loves truffles and mushrooms, and organizes popular "mushroom weekends".

### 2 La Marmite, Rouen

MAP L5 ▪ 3 rue de Florence ▪ 02 35 71 75 55 ▪ Closed Mon & Tue lunch, Sun dinner ▪ €€

An elegant little restaurant, off the tourist track, serving superb gourmet cuisine on a range of menus, including a seven-course *dégustation surprise*.

Le Pavé d'Auge sign

### 3 Hôtel de la Marine, Barneville-Carteret

MAP A3 ▪ 11 rue de Paris ▪ 02 33 53 83 31 ▪ Closed Sun dinner, Mon & Thu lunch (Mar, Oct & Nov); Mon & Thu lunch (Apr–Jun & Sep) ▪ €€€

From his *broche de pigeonneau* to his *soufflé au kalamansi*, Laurent Cesne's blend of innovation and delicacy has won him many admirers. Enjoy panoramic views out to sea from the terrace.

### 4 Le Baligan, Cabourg

MAP E3 ▪ 8 av Alfred Piat ▪ 02 31 24 10 92 ▪ Closed Wed ▪ €

This is an outstanding fish restaurant whose house specialities are fish soup and cod cassoulet. Tables fill up quickly with locals, so book ahead.

### 5 Le Pressoir – Ivan Vautier, Caen

MAP D3 ▪ 3 av Henry-Chéron ▪ 02 31 73 32 71 ▪ Closed Sun dinner, Mon all day, 3 weeks Aug ▪ €€€

This restaurant is one of the best in Caen. Award-winning chef Ivan Vautier creates remarkable dishes paying homage to the best local produce.

### 6 Le Pavé d'Auge, Beuvron-en-Auge

MAP E3 ▪ Pl du Village ▪ 02 31 79 26 71 ▪ Closed Mon, Tue, Dec ▪ €€

The former covered market of this picturesque village is the setting for the Pays d'Auge's most sophisticated restaurant, where dishes featuring ingredients such as langoustines, asparagus and foie gras are served, along with an excellent range of fine wines.

### 7 Manoir de la Drôme, Balleroy

MAP C3 ▪ 129 rue des Forges ▪ 02 31 21 60 94 ▪ Closed Tue lunch, Sun dinner, Mon & Wed all day, mid-Feb–mid-Mar ▪ €€

The garden at this old mill is the ideal spot for an elegant meal. Denis Leclerc's menus are sumptuous, but be ready to leave them aside to try one of the specials created from the best ingredients of the day, such as sole with foie gras.

### 8 Gill, Rouen
MAP G3 ■ 8–9 quai de la Bourse ■ 02 35 71 16 14 ■ Closed Sun, Mon, first 2 weeks Apr & 3 weeks Aug ■ €€€

With its two Michelin stars, Gill is Normandy's foremost gourmet establishment. In the elegant quayside dining room here, the best of Norman produce is beautifully transformed into memorable concoctions such as *pigeon à la rouennaise avec ses raviolis aux herbes*.

### 9 SaQuaNa, Honfleur
MAP F3 ■ 22 pl Hamelin ■ 02 31 89 40 80 ■ Closed Mon–Wed, 1 week late Aug, mid-Jan–late Feb ■ €€€

The name is short for "Saveurs (flavours), Qualité, Nature". Chef Alexandre Bourdas has an adventurous approach, combining Japanese and other influences with the very finest local produce. The decor is modern and very chic.

**Pigeon pastilla at SaQuaNa**

### 10 La Chaîne d'Or, Les Andelys
MAP H3 ■ 25–7 rue Grande ■ 02 32 54 00 31 ■ Closed Tue, Wed & Sun dinner mid-Oct–mid-Apr ■ €€

This 18th-century inn offers excellent traditional cooking and fantastic river views. The *menu dégustation* is very reasonably priced.

**Classic decor at La Chaîne d'Or**

## TOP 10 NORMAN PRODUCE

**Normandy apples and cider**

### 1 Apples and Pears
Normandy's fertile soil supports countless varieties, which are used widely in cooking, and for cider, Calvados and sparkling *poiré*.

### 2 Vegetables
Manche is known for its superb carrots, leeks, radishes, shallots and parsley.

### 3 Dairy Products
The rich milk produced by Norman cattle makes velvety cream, butter (*beurre d'Isigny* is highly prized), and products ranging from Petit-Suisse cream cheese to *confiture de lait* – literally "milk jam".

### 4 Cheese
Four great soft cheeses – Camembert, Pont l'Evêque, Neufchâtel and Livarot – star on the Norman cheese board.

### 5 Agneau de pré-salé
Lamb raised on the salt marshes around Mont-St-Michel has a deliciously delicate flavour.

### 6 Boudin noir
Black pudding is the speciality of Mortagne-au-Perche *(see p81)*.

### 7 Andouille
Also famous is the black tripe sausage produced in Vire.

### 9 Fish
The Atlantic waters yield superb fish, supreme among which is the Dover sole (*sole Normande*).

### 9 Oysters
Norman oysters come from beds in one of three *crus*, or areas: Côte Ouest, St-Vaast-la-Hougue and Isigny.

### 10 Pork
Pale-fleshed Norman pork is a delicacy, particularly *porc de Bayeux*.

*For a key to restaurant price ranges see p91*

# 🔟 Markets

### 1 St-Lô
MAP C4

There's a typical market on Saturday mornings in the main square of this ancient town, where you can buy fresh produce from local farmers and fishermen among the stalls selling furniture, clothing and flowers.

### 2 Caen
MAP D3

Handsome 18th-century houses line place St-Sauveur, the square in the centre of Caen where the pillory once stood, and where the colourful Friday market has been held since 1026. Stallholders sell traditional produce and, for early risers, an amazing selection of fresh fish.

### 3 Dives-sur-Mer
MAP E3

The traditional Saturday market in Dives takes place in the town's spectacular 15th-century timbered *halles* with its red-tiled roof. On Tuesdays in July and August there's a small market of regional products.

### 4 Rouen
MAP G3

Place St-Marc is the scene of a lively market on Tuesday, Friday, Saturday and Sunday, with fresh produce, bric-a-brac and second-hand books. From late November, a Christmas market takes over place de la Cathédrale.

**Flowers at St-Pierre-sur-Dives market**

### 5 St-Pierre-sur-Dives
MAP E4

This inland town has a magnificent covered market hall. Dating from the 11th century, it was the largest medieval hall in Normandy. After it burned down in 1944, it was rebuilt in the style of the original, using hundreds of thousands of wooden pegs instead of screws and nails. Small local producers attend the busy Monday market.

### 6 Dieppe
MAP G1

Each Saturday, from 8am until noon, the long, pedestrian Grande Rue, lined with some 200 shops, becomes a massive open-air emporium.

**Fruit and vegetable stall, Rouen market**

Locals sell their produce (organic fruit and vegetables, *saucisses*, jams), professional retailers bring imports (olives, honey, cheeses) from every corner of France, and fishermen sell their daily catch. Dieppe is famous for its *lisettes* (baby mackerel), scallops and *gendarmes*, the smoked herrings available in November.

### 7 L'Aigle
**MAP F5**

This huge, bustling market draws thousands of people to L'Aigle every Tuesday. Hundreds of stalls, piled high with regional fruits and vegetables, cheeses and cider, are crammed into the town centre. L'Aigle's livestock market (7:30–9:30am), the third largest in France, provides raucous accompaniment.

### 8 Forges-les-Eaux
**MAP H2**

An excellent farmers' market is held on Thursday mornings in the town centre and on Sunday mornings in Halle Baltard in this spa town on the Route du Fromage de Neufchâtel (see p66). Stalls are crammed with organic dairy products, eggs, smoked meat and fish, jam and the Pays de Bray cheeses, including the famous Neufchâtel. On Thursday, there is a livestock market as well.

### 9 Cambremer
**MAP E4**

Local people dressed in peasant costumes, folk dancing, music-making and horse-drawn carriage rides are all part of the fun at Cambremer's market, staged every Sunday morning in July and August and on special occasions such as Easter, 1 May and Whit Sunday. Local producers mingle with regional craftsmen and artists.

### 10 Bayeux
**MAP D3**

One edge of the market that fills place St-Patrice on Saturday mornings is given over to local smallholders selling their own fruit, vegetables, cheese, meats and also livestock (a few geese or chickens). The other stallholders are professional retailers, selling clothes as well as food.

**Saucissons, Bayeux market**

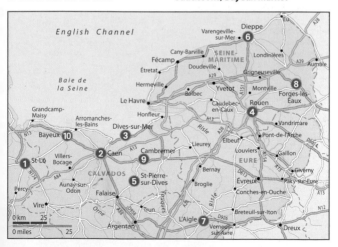

# 🔟 Normandy for Free

**1** **La Pointe du Hoc**
A free visitor centre at La Pointe du Hoc relates the dramatic landings made here by the Americans on D-Day. The site has been preserved unchanged since then and bomb craters still pit the ground *(see p34)*.

**2** **Batterie de Longues-sur-Mer**
The Batterie de Longues-sur-Mer was a German defensive post during the war. Its observation post and guns are still intact, facing out across the Channel. Visitors are welcome to wander around and get a feel for the site *(see p34)*.

**3** **Abbaye Notre-Dame, Le Bec-Hellouin**
Visitors can wander for free around the tranquil grounds of the beautiful Abbaye Notre-Dame in Le Bec-Hellouin. The original medieval monastery – at one time the most influential abbey in Normandy – has largely been rebuilt since its destruction in the French Revolution, but the handsome 15th-century St Nicholas tower and various ruins still remain *(see pp52 & 97)*.

**4** **Château d'O**
Combining Flamboyant Gothic and Renaissance architectural styles, this splendid turreted château is surrounded by a moat, a series of gardens, and stunning parkland. The house is occupied by the family that own it, but guided tours take in the courtyard and some of the grandest 18th-century rooms *(see p113)*.

**Bomb craters on the Pointe du Hoc**

The popular Le Tréport Funicular

**5** **Le Tréport Funicular**
MAP H1 ▪ Open Jul–Aug: 7:45am–12:45am daily; Sep–Jun: 7:45am–8:45pm Sun–Fri
One of the most enjoyable things you can do in the pretty seaside town of Le Tréport *(see p88)* is take the funicular up to the top where you can admire wonderful views of the town and the coast.

**6** **Les Jardins du Pontgirard**
MAP F6 ▪ Monceaux-le-Perche ▪ Open May–Sep: 10am–6pm daily except Wed
The restored gardens of the handsome Manoir du Pontgirard, surrounded by forest in the Perche countryside, are a delight, with their ponds, ancient trees and a wide variety of flowers, including lavender and dozens of types of euphorbia.

### ⑦ Cathédrale de Lumière, Rouen

Show daily: early Jun–July 11pm; first half Aug 10:30pm; second half Aug 10pm; Sep 9:30pm ▪ www.metropole-rouen-normandie.fr

On summer nights, the façade of Rouen cathedral *(see pp24–5)* becomes the backdrop to a spectacular 30-minute video projection. Past themes have included the story of Joan of Arc, the Vikings and Monet.

### ⑧ Fromagerie Graindorge, Livarot

MAP E4 ▪ 42 rue Général-Leclerc ▪ Open Apr–Jun & Sep–Oct: 9:30am–12:30pm & 2:30–5:30pm Mon–Sat; Jul–Aug: 9:30am–5:30pm Mon–Sat; Nov–Mar: 10am–12:30pm & 2:30–5:30pm Mon–Fri, 10am–1pm Sat ▪ 02 31 48 20 00 ▪ www.graindorge.fr

At this long-established *fromagerie*, where Livarot and other Normandy cheeses are made, you can watch the cheese-making process from windows looking out onto the factory (which operates only in the mornings). There is a tasting at the end of the tour.

### ⑨ Aître St-Maclou, Rouen

Built in the 16th century during an outbreak of the plague, the Aître St-Maclou *(see p26)* was a cemetery and charnel house. The courtyard looks very charming until you realize that the beams of the surrounding buildings are decorated with skulls and crossbones and chilling *danse macabre* imagery.

### ⑩ Théâtre Romain de Lillebonne

MAP F2 ▪ Pl Félix Faure 76170 Lillebonne ▪ Jun–mid-Sep: 10am–noon, 2–6pm Sat & Sun ▪ 02 35 15 69 11 ▪ www.theatrelillebonne.fr

Lillebonne, on the banks of the Seine River, was a prosperous Roman port. Its amphitheatre, dating back to the 1st century, was unearthed between 1822 and 1840. The amphitheatre could hold up to 3,000 spectators. Further excavations in 2007 unearthed two more stages.

---

**TOP 10 MONEY-SAVING TIPS**

**Market shopping in Honfleur**

**1** Admission to many museums and sights is free or reduced for under-18s, students and over-60s. In Caen, the free Caen pass from the tourist office gives reductions at a number of museums, restaurants and shops.

**2** Some museums are free on certain days; for example, the Musée des Impressionismes *(see p42)* is free on the first Sunday of the month. State museums are free for EU citizens under 25.

**3** Set lunches at restaurants, especially at the high-end gastronomic establishments, can be very good value and cost less than the popular evening meals.

**4** In Caen, Le Havre and Rouen, buy a carnet of bus/metro tickets rather than purchase individual tickets.

**5** In cafés, you can save money by avoiding the *terrasse*, which is more expensive than sitting at a table inside. Cheapest of all is standing at the bar.

**6** Having breakfast at a café will usually cost less than at your hotel.

**7** Many churches have free recitals and concerts. Tourist offices can provide details of these and other free events taking place in the local area.

**8** Staying in a youth hostel, *chambre d'hôte*, a *ferme-auberge* (farmstay) or apartment can often be quite a bit cheaper than staying in a hotel.

**9** In a restaurant you can cut costs by asking for *eau du robinet* (tap water) and wine or cider by the *pichet* (jug).

**10** Weekly markets, held in many small towns and villages, are very good sources of affordable food, clothes, gifts and bric-a-brac.

# 🔟 Festivals and Events

**Sunset at Rouen's popular boating event L'Armada**

### 1 L'Armada, Rouen
MAP G3 ■ Jun/Jul
■ www.armada.org

In late June/early July every five or six years, Rouen hosts a fleet of tall ships and battleships from across the globe. The city and its environs buzz with festivities and firework displays for eight lively days and nights, culminating in a colourful parade of boats down the Seine. The next Armada takes place in 2019.

### 2 Carnaval de Granville
MAP B5 ■ Feb/Mar ■ Granville tourist office: 02 33 91 30 03

The Carnaval began in the 16th century as a farewell party for local fishermen. Today, people flock from all over France to see the extravagantly decorated floats at this four-day event, starting on the Sunday before Shrove Tuesday.

### 3 Rouen sur Mer
MAP L6 ■ Jun/Jul
■ www.rouen.fr/rsm

For three weeks in July the left bank of the Seine in Rouen is turned into a beach, with imported sand, deckchairs, beach umbrellas, giant waterslides and children's activities. On Friday evenings, there's a live concert.

### 4 Jazz sous les Pommiers, Coutances
MAP B4 ■ May ■ Coutances tourist office: 02 33 19 08 10 ■ www.jazz souslespommiers.com

Jazz sous les Pommiers (Jazz under the Apple Trees) has been running in Coutances for more than 20 years, and each year it grows in size. Over one week in May, it features concerts by established artists, as well as showcasing new talent. There are also promenade concerts, street performances and jam sessions.

**Jazz sous les Pommiers performance**

### ⑤ Foire au Boudin, Mortagne-au-Perche

**MAP F6 ▪ Mar/Apr ▪ Mortagne tourist office: 02 33 83 34 37**

For 40 years, a fair has been held in Mortagne-au-Perche halfway through Lent to celebrate the local gourmet speciality – *boudin noir*, a long sausage made from pig's blood, onions and pork fat. Over three days, butchers gather to sell more than 5 km (3 miles) of this delicacy. Competitions include one to find the person who can eat the most.

### ⑥ Fête des Marins, Honfleur

**MAP F3 ▪ Whit Sunday ▪ Honfleur tourist office: 02 31 89 23 30**

Local fishing boats, specially decorated for the occasion, meet in the Vieux Bassin on Whit Sunday to start their parade, which finishes with a priest's blessing in the Seine estuary. The festival continues the next day when fishermen and sailors march with model ships to Chapelle Notre-Dame de Grâce.

**Spit roasts, Foire de Sainte-Croix**

### ⑦ Foire de Sainte-Croix, Lessay

**MAP B3 ▪ Sep ▪ Lessay tourist office: 02 33 45 14 34**

The date of the first Holy Cross Fair is lost in the mists of time, but it was probably in the 11th century and supported by Benedictine monks. In the 21st century, some 400,000 people gather over three days on the second weekend in September. As well as almost 2,000 exhibitors and livestock sales, there are carnival rides and traditional spit roasts.

**Fans at the Deauville Film Festival**

### ⑧ Festival du Cinéma Américain, Deauville

**MAP E3 ▪ Sep ▪ Deauville tourist office: 02 31 14 40 00 ▪ www.festival-deauville.com**

Although it is not quite as prestigious as Cannes or Venice, this festival dedicated to the best American movies of the year always attracts its share of Hollywood stars. Unsurprisingly, the premieres are the most popular screenings. Awards are presented by an all-French jury.

### ⑨ Le Normandy Horse Show à St-Lô

**MAP C4 ▪ Centre de Promotion de l'Élevage, Haras National, av du Maréchal-Juin ▪ Aug ▪ 02 33 77 88 66**

This major event in the equestrian calendar takes place over one week in August, and includes auctions of horses, ponies and donkeys, as well as numerous competitions. The showjumping and obstacle courses are the most popular. Spectators will see all sorts of different breeds, from sporting to cart horses.

### ⑩ Foire aux Dindes, Sées

**MAP E5 ▪ Dec ▪ Sées tourist office: 02 33 28 74 79**

On the second Saturday in December, the seductive medieval town of Sées is filled with the incongruous sound of gobbling. People come from all over Orne and beyond to Normandy's largest and most important turkey fair, and preview their Christmas dinner.

# Normandy
# Area by Area

Le Vieux Bassin, Honfleur

# 🔟 Northeastern Normandy

**Gros Horloge, an astronomical clock in Rouen**

Inland from the dramatic Côte d'Albâtre, with its harbours and seaside resorts sheltering between chalky cliffs, northeastern Normandy is dominated by the Seine, which follows a meandering course at its southern border. An unspoiled region of forests and rivers, it embraces the *département* of Seine-Maritime and – north of the Seine and reaching to the Epte – a slice of Eure. At the confluence of the two rivers is Giverny, the village made famous by Monet. Seine-Maritime has a varied landscape with the lush, sparsely populated Pays de Bray in the northeast and, at its heart, the limestone plateau of the Pays de Caux. Between the sea and the cultured cathedral city of Rouen, one magnificent abbey after another overlooks the wooded banks of the Seine Valley – spiritual stations on the well-trodden Abbey Route.

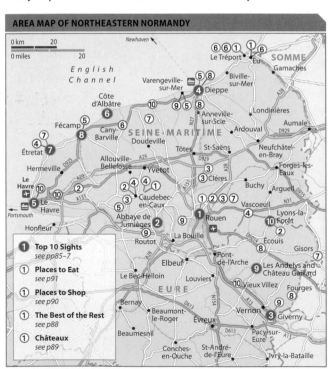

**AREA MAP OF NORTHEASTERN NORMANDY**

1 **Top 10 Sights**
see pp85–7

1 **Places to Eat**
see p91

1 **Places to Shop**
see p90

1 **The Best of the Rest**
see p88

1 **Châteaux**
see p89

**The Seine winding through the historic city of Rouen**

### 1 Rouen

Founded by the Romans in around 50 BC, the capital of Haute-Normandie occupied a strategic site on the Seine – the last point where the river could be bridged. From the end of the Hundred Years' War, Rouen prospered through textile production and maritime trade. The north bank's treasures – including streets of half-timbered houses and the magnificent cathedral – attract thousands of visitors (see pp24–6).

### 2 Abbaye de Jumièges

The remains of this 7th-century abbey, which housed 900 monks, but was reduced to ruins in the Revolution, are stunning (see pp22–3).

### 3 Giverny

Pay homage to Monet in his own home, the Fondation Claude Monet, and wander in the garden that inspired him. The Musée des Impressionnismes explores the history of Impressionism and Post-Impressionism (see pp40–43).

### 4 Dieppe

MAP G1 ■ Tourist office: pont Jehan Ango, quai du Carénage ■ 02 32 14 40 60

The first beach resort in France, Dieppe occupies a striking position between limestone cliffs. As a Channel port, it was coveted for centuries by foreign invaders, and has long been a favourite with British tourists, for its sweeping beach and lively old town centred on the Grande Rue (see p76).

Nearby, Église St-Jacques has a memorial to the thousands of Canadians killed in Operation Jubilee in 1942. Above the town, the medieval castle is now a museum, with a fine Impressionist collection and some remarkable 16th-century carved ivory. Dieppe's other engaging museum is the Cité de la Mer, with aquariums and exhibits on maritime history.

**Boats moored at Dieppe harbour**

### 5 Le Havre

MAP E2 ■ Tourist office: 186 bd Clémenceau ■ 02 32 74 04 04

Founded in 1517 to replace the silted-up ports of Honfleur, Harfleur and Caudebec, Le Havre is now France's second port and a UNESCO World Heritage Site, a tribute to its recovery from the bombing that flattened it in 1944. One of the few survivors is the 16th-century cathedral, a hybrid of Gothic and Renaissance styles. The city was rebuilt to designs by Auguste Perret, and the starkly imposing Église St-Joseph is typical of his style. More modern is the glass, aluminium and steel structure housing the Musée Malraux (see p55).

### 6 Côte d'Albâtre
MAP E2, F1, G1, H1

On first sight of the Alabaster Coast, you might think that you were across the Channel: it bears a striking resemblance to the White Cliffs of Dover. Stretching southwest from Le Tréport to Le Havre, the coastline is pitted by *valleuses* – dry hanging valleys in the clifftops, revealed as the cliffs retreat before the combined forces of sea and weather. Harbours shelter in natural shingle inlets, while larger towns cluster on the estuaries. This coast offers some of the region's most spectacular scenery.

**View of Falaise d'Aval from Étretat**

### 7 Étretat
Nestling between two cliffs, Falaises d'Aval and d'Amont, this picturesque village was a sleepy place until the 19th-century onslaught of writers, painters and Parisian holiday-makers. For the best view of Falaise d'Aval – an extraordinary rock formation with a natural arch – climb to Notre-Dame-de-la-Garde, the mariners' chapel atop Falaise d'Amont. Nearby, a monument commemorates aviators Nungesser and Coli, whose aeroplane was last seen near here on the first, failed attempt to fly the Atlantic in 1927. In Étretat itself, visit Place Foch, where 16th-century houses cluster around timbered *halles* – an attractive 1920s reconstruction of a covered market – and admire the town's stunning *belle époque* mansions (see pp30–31).

**THE SEINE**

The second-longest, busiest and most famous river in France, the Seine has its source in Burgundy, flows through Paris, and finally meets the sea at Le Havre. Its lower course through Normandy is wide enough to accommodate large ships and barges: hence its historical importance for settlers and invaders, and the location of Rouen and the Norman abbeys.

### 8 Fécamp
MAP F2 ■ Tourist office: quai Sadi-Carnot ■ 02 35 28 51 01

After a casket said to contain precious drops of Christ's blood was washed ashore in the 1st century, Fécamp became a pilgrimage centre. First an abbey (now ruined) was built to house the holy relic, after which the glorious Abbatiale de la Trinité was erected in the 12th to 13th centuries (see p52). More prosaically, the cornerstone of this no-nonsense fishing port has been the humble cod. Fécamp's other claim to fame is as the birthplace of the herbal liqueur Bénédictine, first concocted in 1863 by merchant Alexandre le Grand, using an old monastic recipe. It continues to be distilled in his overblown 19th-century Gothic Palais Bénédictine, which contains laboratories, a museum and gallery, and offers tastings (see p90).

**Palais Bénédictine, Fécamp**

**Atmospheric Château Gaillard**

### ⑨ Les Andelys and Château Gaillard

MAP H3 ■ Tourist office: rue Raymond Phelip ■ 02 32 54 41 93

The twin villages of Grand and Petit Andelys enjoy a glorious setting on a lazy curve of the Seine in the shadow of the pale ruins of Richard the Lionheart's Château Gaillard, built at break-neck speed in 1196 to prevent Philippe Auguste from reaching Rouen. Below lie the winding streets of tranquil, timbered Petit Andely, and more commercial Grand Andely, with a grand 16th- to 17th-century church and a couple of interesting museums – one dedicated to the painter Nicolas Poussin, the other to the Normandie-Niémen regiment.

### ⑩ Lyons-la-Forêt

MAP H3 ■ Tourist office: 20 rue de l'Hôtel de Ville ■ 02 32 49 31 65

Visit this picture-postcard town in the Lieure Valley and you'll understand why Maurice Ravel used to come here to compose. Sights nearby include the impressive early 17th-century pink-brick Château de Fleury-la-Forêt, with a superb collection of toys and dolls; Château de Vascoeuil, which has traditional cottages and modern sculpture in its grounds; and the ruined Cistercian Abbaye de Mortemer, with its museum.

---

**A DRIVE THROUGH THE VAL DE SEINE**

### ▶ MORNING

Take the D982 from Rouen to St-Martin-de-Boscherville to visit the lovely Romanesque abbey of **St-Georges de Boscherville** (see p88). Walk around the gardens and enjoy the views. After a browse in the abbey shop, revive yourself at one of the village bars.

Continue on the D982 until you reach the D143 turn-off for the bewitching, ruined **Abbaye de Jumièges** (see pp22–3). This is a place for calm contemplation, so don't rush your visit. Afterwards, make your way to the picturesque Seine-side inn **Auberge du Bac** (2 rue Alphonse Callais) for lunch.

#### AFTERNOON

From Jumièges, cross over the river by *bac* (ferryboat) into the Forêt de Brotonne (see p63) in the **Parc Naturel Régional des Boucles de la Seine Normande** (see p60). Spend some time exploring this tranquil forest, which boasts one of the largest concentrations of beech trees in France. Cross the elegant **Pont de Brotonne** over to the town of **Caudebac-en-Caux** (see p88) and admire its splendid Flamboyant Gothic church and medieval Maison des Templiers.

Then take the D81 on to the delightful little riverside town of **Villequier** (see p88). Enjoy a walk along the promenade here and watch the boats go by, before heading for dinner at **Le Manoir de Rétival** (see p91), or the **Grand Sapin** (12 rue Jean le Gaffric), with its lovely Seine-side setting.

*See map on p84* ←

# The Best of the Rest

### 1 Le Tréport
MAP H1 ■ Tourist office: quai Sadi Carnot ■ 02 35 86 05 69

This popular seaside town is famous for its smoked fish *(see p90)*, and also for the view of the coast from the Calvaire (calvary) above the town.

### 2 Caudebec-en-Caux
MAP G2 ■ Tourist office: pl du Général de Gaulle ■ 02 32 70 46 32

A jaunty Seine-side town with a centuries-old Saturday market, Flamboyant Gothic church and medieval Templar's house.

### 3 Villequier
MAP F2 ■ Musée Victor-Hugo: open 10am–12:30pm, 2–5:30pm Mon, Wed–Sat, 2–5:30pm Sun; Adm charge

Set in a beautiful spot on the Seine, Villequier marks the point where river becomes estuary. Victor Hugo's daughter Léopoldine drowned here in 1843. The Musée Victor-Hugo commemorates her life.

### 4 Abbaye de St-Wandrille
MAP G2 ■ Guided tours: phone 02 35 96 23 11 for details

The chequered history of this working Benedictine monastery goes back to 649, and even includes a spell as home to the Marquis of Stackpole in the 19th century.

### 5 Varengeville-sur-Mer
MAP G1

Gloriously situated, its clifftop church has windows by Ubac and Braques. Lutyens and Jekyll collaborated on the nearby Parc du Bois des Moutiers *(see p65)*.

### 6 Eu
MAP H1 ■ Tourist office: pl Guillaume le Conquérant ■ 02 35 86 04 68

This handsome riverside town is named after the Irish Archbishop St Lawrence (Lorcán Ua – or Eu – Tuathail), who died here in 1180.

Ruins of the castle in Gisors

### 7 Gisors
MAP J3 ■ Tourist office: 4 rue du Général de Gaulle ■ 02 32 27 60 63

In the capital of Norman Vexin, a fine 13th- to 14th-century church keeps company with the imposing castle William the Conqueror constructed to protect his borders.

### 8 Écouis
MAP H3 ■ Abbaye de Fontaine Guérard: Fleury-sur-Andelle; open Apr–Oct: pm Tue–Sun; Adm charge

The heart of Écouis is the church of Notre-Dame, built in 1313. The nearby ruined 12th-century Abbaye de Fontaine Guérard is worth a short excursion.

### 9 Abbaye St-Georges de Boscherville
MAP G3 ■ St-Martin-de-Boscherville ■ Open Apr–Oct: 9am–6:30pm daily; Nov–Mar: 2–5pm daily ■ Adm charge

This is an exquisite example of Norman Romanesque architecture, complete with intricate carvings.

Carving at Boscherville

### 10 Veules-les-Roses
MAP G1 ■ Tourist office: 27 rue Victor Hugo ■ 02 35 97 63 05

In its own valley, at the mouth of France's shortest river, this pretty village clusters around a 12th-century church.

# Châteaux

**1 Château d'Eu**
MAP H1 ■ Eu ■ Open mid-Mar–
Oct: 10am–noon & 2–6pm Wed–Mon
(Fri pm only) ■ Adm charge

Queen Victoria came to stay in Louis
Philippe's 16th-century holiday
home. It is now the Musée Louis-
Philippe, crammed with antiques.

**2 Château de Filières**
MAP F2 ■ Gommerville ■ 02 35
20 53 30 ■ Open May–Jun & Sep:
2–6pm Sat, Sun & hols; Jul–Aug
2–6pm daily ■ Adm charge

The left wing is all that remains of the
original Henri IV house. The park's
beech avenue is dubbed La Cathédrale
because it resembles Gothic vaults.

**3 Château de Clères**
MAP G2 ■ Clères ■ 02 35 33 23
08 ■ Open Apr–Sep: 10am–7pm daily;
Oct: 10am–noon & 1:30–6:30pm daily
■ Adm charge

This impressive château has extensive
gardens that harbour a small zoo. It
also hosts temporary art exhibitions.

**4 Château de Vascoeuil**
MAP H3 ■ Vascoeuil ■ 02 35 23
62 35 ■ Open Apr–Jun, Sep–Oct: 2:30–
6pm Wed–Sun (Jul, Aug: 10:30am–1pm,
2:30–6:30pm daily) ■ Adm charge

There are more than 50 sculptures
throughout the grounds here.

**5 Château d'Ételan**
MAP F3 ■ St-Maurice-d'Ételan
■ 02 35 39 91 27 ■ Open mid-Jun–mid-
Jul & Sep: 3–7pm Sat & Sun; mid-Jul–
Aug: 3–7pm Sat–Tue ■ Adm charge

A striking example of the 15th-
century Flamboyant Gothic, this
château has a jewel of a chapel.

**6 Château de Cany-Barville**
MAP F2 ■ Cany ■ Open Jul–
Aug: 10am–noon & 3–6pm Sat–Thu
■ Adm charge

Built by François Mansart (whose
uncle built Versailles) in the 1640s,
this impressive moated château, has
always been in the same family.

**7 Château du Mesnil-
Geoffroy**
MAP G1 ■ Ermenouville ■ 02 35 57 12
77 ■ Open May–Sep: 2:30–6pm Wed–
Sun & hols ■ Adm charge

This 17th-century house of brick
and stone has extensive grounds
with a wonderful hornbeam maze by
Le Nôtre gardener Colinet, a pretty
rose garden and a kitchen garden.

**8 Château de Miromesnil**
MAP G1 ■ Tourville-sur-Arques
■ Apr–Oct: 10am–noon & 2–6pm
daily ■ Adm charge

Visit the Montebello salon and the
Marquis de Miromesnil's rooms in
the 16th- to 17th-century mansion
where the famous writer Guy de
Maupassant was born. The landscaped
park and walled gardens have been
classified as a Jardin Remarquable.

**Château de Miromesnil**

**9 Manoir d'Ango**
MAP G1 ■ Varengeville-sur-
Mer ■ 02 35 83 61 56 ■ Open Easter–
end Sep: 10am–12:30pm & 2–6pm
daily; Oct: Sat, Sun & public hols
■ Adm charge

Built in the 16th century, this is a
glorious Italian Renaissance manor.

**10 Château d'Orcher**
MAP F2 ■ Gonfreville l'Orcher
■ 02 35 45 45 91 ■ Open Jul–mid-
Aug: 2–6pm Tue–Sun ■ Adm charge

This 11th-century fort (remodelled in
the 18th century) has a spectacular
clifftop setting and a sweeping park
with pretty avenues of ash trees.

*See map on p84* ←

# Places to Shop

### 1 Abbaye de St-Wandrille
MAP G2

A 14th-century barn houses the shop of the famous abbey (see p52 & p88). This is the main outlet for the monks' products, including CDs of Gregorian chant, honey, and beeswax candles.

### 2 Faïencerie Augy, Rouen
MAP M5 ■ 26 rue St-Romain ■ 02 35 88 77 47

Attractive plates, jugs, vases and lamps are decorated and fired according to 16th-century methods in the workshops attached to this seductive faïence shop. You can see demonstrations by appointment.

### 3 La Chocolatière, Rouen
MAP L5 ■ 18 rue Guillaume le Conquérant

A haven for chocolate lovers, this sleek grey shop's signature treat is the deliciously decadent Rouen speciality *paillardises* (rich praline-layered chocolates).

### 4 Manoir de Cateuil
MAP F2 ■ Rte du Havre

This lovely domain near Étretat produces home-made ciders and goat's cheese, as well as some tasty ice creams and chocolate made with fresh goat's milk.

### 5 Palais Bénédictine, Fécamp
MAP F2 ■ 110 rue Alexandre-le-Grand ■ Closed Jan–early Feb

Taste the liqueur, aged in casks in the palace basement, before visiting the shop, well stocked with bottles of Bénédictine and B&B (Bénédictine blended with brandy).

### 6 Delgove et Cie, Le Tréport
MAP H1 ■ Parc Sainte-Croix

Using the traditional local method of smoking fish (drying in sawdust before smoking over a beechwood fire), this smoke-house sells salmon, mackerel, herring and haddock.

### 7 Caves Bérigny, Rouen
MAP L5 ■ 7 rue Rollon ■ 02 35 07 57 54 ■ Open am Tue–Sat

French wines and the best Normandy ciders and Calvados line the shelves at this attractive shop. There are also branches in Fécamp, Lillebonne and Le Havre.

### 8 L'Epicier Olivier, Dieppe
MAP G1 ■ 18 rue St-Jacques ■ 02 35 84 22 55 ■ Open Tue–Sat (Jul & Aug: also Mon pm)

Every kind of French gourmet product is stocked here: charcuterie and cheeses, fine coffees, mustards, spices, oils and preserves. There's also a magnificent selection of fine wines, ciders and liqueurs.

Cheeses at L'Epicier Olivier, Dieppe

### 9 Maison du Lin, Routot
MAP G3 ■ Pl du Général-Leclerc ■ 02 32 56 21 76 ■ Open Mar & Oct: 2–6pm Sat & Sun; Apr–Jun & Sep: 2–6pm Wed–Mon; Jul–Aug: 2–6pm daily

Learn about the history and production of linen at this museum, then treat yourself to some napkins or a tea towel.

### 10 Saveur Chocolat, Le Havre
MAP F2 ■ 19 rue Albert André-Huet

The Auzou family have been *chocolatiers* since 1961. Their shop is *the* place to buy "Tears of Joan of Arc" (chocolate-covered almonds).

# Places to Eat

**PRICE CATEGORIES**
For a three-course meal for one with half
a bottle of wine (or equivalent meal),
taxes and extra charges.

€ under €40  €€ €40–€60  €€€ over €60

**1 Le P'tit Bec, Rouen**
MAP N5 ▪ 182 rue Eau de Robec
▪ 02 35 07 63 33 ▪ Closed Sun ▪ €

The warm and friendly Le P'tit Bec
serves dependable dishes such as
*confit de canard* (duck confit), plus a
mouthwatering range of gratins.

**2 La Licorne Royale,
Lyons-la-Forêt**
MAP H3 ▪ 27 pl Benserade ▪ 02 32
48 24 24 ▪ Closed Mon–Fri lunch,
Wed ▪ €€€

The restaurant of the Hôtel de la
Licorne creatively combines rustic
charm with modern cuisine.

**3 Au Souper Fin,
Frichemesnil**
MAP H2 ▪ 1 rte de Clères ▪ 02 35 33 33
88 ▪ Closed Sun dinner, Wed, Thu ▪ €€€

This snug restaurant is the perfect
place to sample Eric Buisset's
inventive, Michelin-starred cooking.

**4 Le Manoir de Rétival,
Caudebec-en-Caux**
MAP G2 ▪ 2 rue St-Clair ▪ 06 50 23
43 63 ▪ €€€

Chef David Görne offers a different
tasting menu every day. Book ahead.

**5 Bistrot du Pollet, Dieppe**
MAP G1 ▪ 23 rue Tête-de-Boeuf
▪ 02 35 84 68 57 ▪ Closed Sun, Mon ▪ €

Slightly out of the way, this little
bistro can put fish on your table
minutes after it has been caught.

**6 Homard Bleu, Le Tréport**
MAP H1 ▪ 45 quai François 1er
▪ 02 35 86 15 89 ▪ €

Wonderful seafood platters, lobster
and fresh fish are the speciality here.
Book ahead for an upstairs table with
views of the harbour. Excellent service.

Interior of Domaine St-Clair, Étretat

**7 Domaine St-Clair,
Étretat**
MAP F2 ▪ Chemin de St-Clair
▪ 02 35 27 08 23 ▪ €€€

Dine by candlelight at this elegant
restaurant housed in a dramatically
located seaside hotel. Chef Wilfrid
Chaplain offers three fixed-price
menus in addition to a good
selection of à la carte dishes.

**8 Le Moulin de Fourges,
Fourges**
MAP J4 ▪ 38 rue du Moulin
▪ 02 32 52 12 12 ▪ Closed Nov–mid-
Mar, Sun dinner, Mon ▪ €€

A pretty mill on the bank of the Epte
offers memorable regional cuisine in
a great setting. Fresh produce is
prepared with skill and imagination.

**9 Restaurant Baudy,
Giverny**
MAP H4 ▪ 81 rue Claude Monet ▪ 02
32 21 10 03 ▪ Closed Nov–Mar ▪ €

The classic bistro lunches served
here make a great accompaniment
to any visit to Monet's garden.

**10 La Closerie, Vieux Villez**
MAP H3 ▪ 17 rue de l'Église
▪ 02 32 77 44 77 ▪ €

Located in the grounds of the
Château Corneille, La Closerie offers
regional specialities, a wide range
of wines and two creative set menus
based on locally sourced ingredients
such as crab and lamb.

*See map on p84* ←

# 🔟 Central Normandy

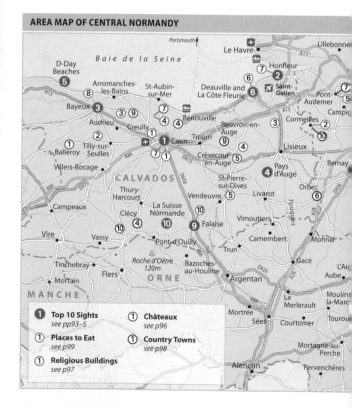

Encompassing the whole of the *département* of Calvados and much of Eure, this region is the true heart of Normandy. From the earthly pleasures of Deauville to the heavenly aspirations of St Thérèse's Lisieux, from the rural idyll of the Pays d'Auge to the architectural magnificence of the Château de Beaumesnil, and from the Bayeux Tapestry to the Impressionist paintings inspired by the enchanting seaport of Honfleur, central Normandy is brimming with variety and interest. William the Conqueror – born in Falaise, buried in Caen – dominates the region's history, as do the bloody events of D-Day, 6 June 1944, and the subsequent Battle of Normandy, played out on its wide, sandy beaches and in its attractive, historic and now carefully restored towns.

**Exhibit from Musée d'Évreux**

## AREA MAP OF CENTRAL NORMANDY

1 **Top 10 Sights**
see pp93–5

1 **Places to Eat**
see p99

1 **Religious Buildings**
see p97

1 **Châteaux**
see p96

1 **Country Towns**
see p98

## 1 Caen

**MAP D3** ■ **Tourist office:**
**pl St-Pierre** ■ **02 31 27 14 14**

Reconstructed after the war, Caen retains its compact historic centre and Romanesque masterpieces, including William the Conqueror's abbey church of St-Étienne, which sheltered hundreds of citizens during the ferocious Battle of Caen in 1944. Many visitors head straight for the absorbing Mémorial museum on the outskirts (see p54) and then leave, but it is worth spending time in this lively, cultured city.

## 2 Honfleur

The highlight of Normandy's coast is this enchanting port, fortified during the Hundred Years' War when it was fought over by the French and the English. Today, it is celebrated for

**Honfleur's picturesque harbour**

both the intrepid mariners who set sail from its harbour and the artists who found inspiration here. The special light of the estuary is at its best just after dawn (see pp20–21).

## 3 Bayeux

Known the world over for its famous tapestry, the small-scale cathedral town itself is less well known – yet full of charm. Allow two hours for a visit to the tapestry in the Centre Guillaume-le-Conquérant, and at least another two hours to explore Vieux Bayeux (see pp16–19).

**A scene from the Bayeux Tapestry**

## 4 Pays d'Auge

If Normandy's coastline reaches a peak of loveliness between Cabourg and Honfleur, then so does the landscape beyond. This is the Pays d'Auge, rich in orchards and dairy farms, which stretches back from the coast through the heart of the *département* of Calvados. Lisieux, famed for its connections with St Thérèse, is its principal town, and there are many old manors and pretty villages to explore, too – as well as cheese, cider and Calvados to taste and buy (see pp38–9).

## 5 D-Day Beaches

Over 70 years after D-Day, the momentous events of 6 June 1944, when the Allies landed on the beaches of the Seine Bay, are commemorated in moving memorials, museums and cemeteries (see pp34–7).

## 6 Deauville and La Côte Fleurie

Normandy's most alluring stretch of coast, fringed by marvellous sandy beaches, is enlivened by a string of resorts that offer something for everyone: gambling (or, if you can't afford to gamble, people-watching) in opulent Deauville; shrimping and sand-yachting in Houlgate and Cabourg; and the many amusements of happy-go-lucky Trouville. The D513 follows the coast, dipping inland around the impressive corniche, Falaises des Vaches Noires, that rises up between Houlgate and Villers-sur-Mer (see pp32–3).

Château d'Anet, Vallée de l'Eure

## 7 Vallée de l'Eure

MAP H4 ■ Tourist office: pl Dufay, Pacy-sur-Eure ■ 02 32 26 18 21

Easily accessible from Paris, the lush Eure Valley is a popular weekend destination for city dwellers. The stretch of the Eure between Chartres and the Seine is sometimes referred to as the Valley of the Mistresses, since it passes first the château of Louis XIV's secret wife, Madame de Maintenon (just outside Normandy in Île de France), then Château d'Anet (see p96), commissioned by Diane de Poitiers, mistress of Henri II. From Anet, the D143 and D836 follow the

river past Ivry-la-Bataille and Pacy-sur-Eure, with its fine 13th-century church. A lovely stretch at Cocherel comes next, then Château d'Acquigny, set in a park. The Eure ends at Louviers, which has a small but pretty old quarter near its 13th-century church of Notre-Dame (see p97).

## 8 Évreux

MAP H4 ■ Tourist office: 1 pl Général-de-Gaulle ■ 02 32 24 04 43

Capital of the *département* of Eure, Évreux has had a turbulent history and more than its fair share of siege and invasion since the Vandals first sacked it in the 5th century. Damaged during World War II, its centre has been rebuilt, with enjoyable gardens and riverside walks. In the Cathédrale de Notre-Dame, Renaissance carvings round the north door date from the height of the Flamboyant period, as do the leaf and flower motifs in the transept and the lantern tower. The Musée d'Évreux includes Gallo-Roman archaeological finds, plus fine medieval misericords and tapestries.

## 9 Falaise

MAP E4 ■ Tourist office: pl Guillaume le Conquérant ■ 02 31 90 17 26

The dashing equestrian statue of William the Conqueror sets the tone in the main square of this attractive town. Falaise is dominated by the vast Château Guillaume-le-Conquérant, birthplace of William in 1027. In August 1944, it was the site of the fierce and decisive Battle of the Mortain-Falaise Pocket. In the

**Château Guillaume-le-Conquérant**

valley below, a modern sculpture recalls the spot where William's father, Robert the Magnificent, saw his future wife washing clothes in the stream. Also worth a visit are Automates Avenue, a collection of 20th-century Parisian shop window automata, and Musée André Lemaitre, with a collection dedicated to this famous locally born artist.

## ⑩ La Suisse Normande
MAP D4–5 ■ Tourist office: 2 pl St-Sauveur, Thury-Harcourt ■ 02 31 79 70 45

This striking region is as close to resembling Switzerland as Normandy gets, and very different from the typical Norman landscape. On its winding northwesterly course, the River Orne has cut through the *massif*, creating steep banks and the occasional severe peak. None of the "heights" are particularly high, but they provide some dizzying views – and plenty of scope for outdoor pursuits. Many come for the canoeing, walking, fishing or rock-climbing; others to hang-glide off the Pain de Sucre. Another high point is the craggy Roche d'Oëtre, with stunning views over the Rouvre gorges. Thury-Harcourt, Pont-d'Ouilly and Clécy (see p98) are the main centres.

**Climbing in La Suisse Normande**

A DRIVE ALONG THE RISLE

### ▶ MORNING

Starting in **Pont-Audemer** (see p98), follow the signposted trail around the town's highlights. On a Friday (market day), rue de la République is always lined with a tempting array of food stalls.

Take the D130 for the lovely 24-km (15-mile) drive along the Risle and through the Fôret de Montfort to **Le Bec-Hellouin** (see pp52 & 78). Wander in the abbey grounds and tour the abbey with a monk as your guide. The village (see p57) is a perfect spot for lunch. If you have a picnic, head back to Pont-Authou, just north of Le Bec-Hellouin, and follow signs over a footbridge to Canoe-Kayak-La Risle, a tranquil spot on an island in the river.

### AFTERNOON

Leave Le Bec-Hellouin on the scenic D39 to St-Martin-du-Parc and Le Buhot, then turn left on the D26 to **Harcourt**, with its stern medieval fortress-château and the oldest arboretum in France (see p96). Leaving by the D137, reconnect with the Risle at **Brionne** (see p98). There's plenty to do here, including canoeing or renting a pedalo. The square *donjon* (keep) on its hill is a fine sight against the setting sun and gives a wonderful panoramic view over the Risle Valley.

In town, there's a choice of cafés and restaurants for a relaxing evening drink or a meal. The best is the 18th-century **Auberge du Vieux Donjon** (rue Soie).

See map on pp92–3 ←

# Châteaux

## ① Château de Balleroy
MAP C3 ▪ 02 31 21 60 61
▪ Open Easter–Jun, Sep–mid-Oct: Wed–Mon; Jul–Aug: daily ▪ Adm charge

Portraits of Napoleon and Wellington confront one another in the Waterloo Room of this sumptuous 16th-century château. A fascinating hot-air balloon museum is also housed in the stables.

Château de Beaumesnil and gardens

## ② Château de Beaumesnil
MAP G4 ▪ 02 32 44 40 09
▪ Open May: pm Sat & Sun; Jun–Aug: daily; Sep: pm Tue–Sun ▪ Adm charge

This glorious Baroque masterpiece, a frothy pile of pink brick and pale stone on a glassy moat, is perfectly complemented by the lovely formal gardens that surround it.

## ③ Château d'Anet
MAP H4 ▪ 02 37 41 90 07
▪ Open Apr–Oct: pm Wed–Mon; Nov–Mar: pm Sat & Sun ▪ Adm charge

Now but a glimmer of its former glory, this château still impresses. Make sure you visit the two chapels.

## ④ Château de Bénouville
MAP D3 ▪ 02 31 95 53 23
▪ Phone for hours ▪ Adm charge

The monumental staircase is the star at this impressive yet charming Neo-Classical château.

## ⑤ Château de Crèvecoeur
MAP E4 ▪ Crèvecœur-en-Auge
▪ 02 31 63 02 45 ▪ Open Apr–Jun & Sep: 11am–6pm daily; Jul–Aug: 11am–7pm daily ▪ Adm charge

A castle, reached by a footbridge, survives at the heart of this complex, which includes a lovely dovecote.

## ⑥ Château de Champ-de-Bataille, Le Neubourg
MAP G4 ▪ Open Easter–Jun & Oct: 2:30–5:30pm Sat & Sun; Jul–Aug: 2:30–5:30pm daily ▪ Adm charge

This 17th-century château is owned by interior designer Jacques Garcia. On view are the kitchens, and lavish gardens inspired by mythology.

## ⑦ Château de Fontaine-Henry
MAP D3 ▪ 02 31 26 93 67
▪ Open Apr–mid-Jun & mid-Sep–Oct: pm Sat & Sun; mid-Jun–mid-Sep: pm Wed–Mon ▪ Adm charge

The huge sloping roofs of this extraordinary Renaissance château are actually taller than its walls.

## ⑧ Le Domaine d'Harcourt
MAP G4 ▪ 02 32 46 29 70
▪ Open mid-Jun–mid-Sep: daily; Mar–mid-Jun, mid-Sep–mid-Nov: pm Wed–Mon ▪ Adm charge

This medieval moated castle is the ancestral home of the Harcourt family, and has an arboretum, created in 1802.

## ⑨ Château de Creully
MAP D3 ▪ 02 31 80 18 65
▪ Open Jul–Aug: Tue–Fri ▪ Adm charge

In the same family since 1613, this château has retained its Louis XIII decoration. It was from here that the BBC reported on the D-Day landings.

## ⑩ Château de Pontécoulant
MAP D4 ▪ 02 31 69 62 54 ▪ Open mid-Mar–mid-Nov: Tue–Sun ▪ Adm charge

This 16th- to 18th-century château in the Suisse Normande has long, formal lawns, backed by woodland.

# Religious Buildings

### 1 Abbaye d'Ardennes, Caen
MAP D3

During the Battle of Normandy, 23 Canadian soldiers were executed at this 12th-century abbey on the town's outskirts; a memorial garden commemorates them. The partially ruined church is a fine example of Norman Gothic architecture.

### 2 Abbaye St-Martin-de-Mondaye, Juaye-Mondaye
MAP D3

The monks of this small community welcome guests on retreat, and host summer concerts in their handsome 18th-century abbey.

### 3 Prieuré de St-Gabriel, Brécy
MAP D3

Set around a courtyard, the lovely honey-stone buildings of this former daughter house of Le Trinité in Fécamp (see p52) are now occupied by a horticultural school. They can be viewed from the outside only.

### 4 St-Pierre, Thaon
MAP D3

No longer in use, this 12th-century church is a lovely sight in its secluded setting, hidden by greenery at the tip of a valley. A real gem of Romanesque architecture.

### 5 Église Abbatiale, St-Pierre-sur-Dives
MAP E4

The copper strip on the nave's floor shows the position of the sun's rays at this large church, once part of an abbey (see p38).

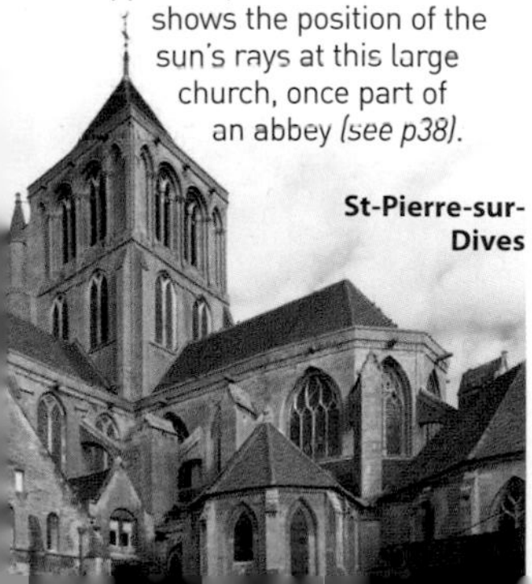

**St-Pierre-sur-Dives**

### 6 Ste-Foy, Conches-en-Ouche
MAP G4

This Flamboyant Gothic church has some of the finest stained glass in Normandy (see p98). Its spire is a copy of one destroyed in a storm in 1842.

### 7 Abbaye-aux-Hommes, Caen
MAP L2

This Romanesque abbey (see p53) was built by William the Conqueror. Guided tours reveal the rest of the abbey complex, including the lovely cloister.

**Abbaye-aux-Hommes, Caen**

### 8 Abbaye Notre-Dame, Le Bec-Hellouin
MAP G3

There is a marvellous view of the abbey as you enter the village from the south. The refectory has been converted into a simple church, where its founder lies buried beneath the altar (see pp52 & 78).

### 9 Notre-Dame, Louviers
MAP H3

From the 13th century, Louviers was an important centre of cloth-making. Its lavishly decorated church reflects the town's former prosperity.

### 10 Notre-Dame, Verneuil-sur-Avre
MAP G5

Built of a reddish stone called *grison*, this church is noted for its plethora of 16th-century statues (see p98).

See map on pp92–3 ←

# Country Towns

**Ruins at Beaumont-le-Roger**

## 1 Beaumont-le-Roger
MAP G4 ■ Tourist office:
1 pl de Clercq ■ 02 32 44 05 79

The stark ruins of the 13th-century priory and the parish church of St-Nicolas are the main sights in this riverside town.

## 2 Bernay
MAP F4 ■ Tourist office:
29 rue Thiers ■ 02 32 43 32 08

Bernay has some picturesque timbered houses (look for rue Gaston-Follope, lined with antiques shops), a museum, and an abbey church begun in 1013.

## 3 Brionne
MAP G3 ■ Tourist office: 1 rue du Général-de-Gaulle ■ 02 32 45 70 51

An excellent base for exploring the Risle Valley, this small market town is overlooked by an 11th-century keep.

## 4 Clécy
MAP D4 ■ Tourist office: pl du Tripot ■ 02 31 79 70 45

This pretty, stone-built village in La Suisse Normande *(see p60 & p95)* boasts a model railway *(see p68)* and a range of holiday activities.

## 5 Conches-en-Ouche
MAP G4 ■ Tourist office:
pl Briand ■ 02 32 30 76 42

Set above a bend in the River Rouloir, Conches has a number of medieval houses and a church that is home to some fine stained-glass windows.

## 6 Orbec
MAP F4 ■ Tourist office:
6 rue Grande ■ 02 31 32 56 68

This delightful country town has many fine old buildings, including the 1563 Vieux Manoir in rue Grande.

## 7 Pont-Audemer
MAP F3 ■ Tourist office: pl du Gén de Gaulle ■ 02 32 41 08 21

Amid nondescript surroundings, Pont-Audemer's charming centre is filled with half-timbered houses.

## 8 Verneuil-sur-Avre
MAP G5 ■ Tourist office: 129 pl de la Madeleine ■ 02 32 32 17 17

This town on the old Franco-Norman border is famous for the chequered brickwork of its buildings, the 13th-century Tour Grise, and the striking tower of Église de la Madeleine.

## 9 Beuvron-en-Auge
MAP E3 ■ Tourist office: 16 rue Pasteur, Cambremer ■ 02 31 63 08 87

Arguably the prettiest village in the Pays d'Auge, Beuvron-en-Auge is full of half-timbered houses, gift shops and good restaurants *(see p38 & p56)*.

## 10 Cormeilles
MAP F3 ■ Tourist office: 21 pl du Général de Gaulle ■ 02 32 56 02 39

Cormeilles suffered relatively little war damage. It has a Friday market and a great Calvados distillery *(see p39)*.

**A historic street in Cormeilles**

# Places to Eat

### ① Le Pressoir, Caen
MAP D3 ▪ 3 av Henry Cheron
▪ 02 31 73 32 71 ▪ Closed Sun dinner,
Mon ▪ €€

Ivan Vautier has a Michelin star for
his innovative take on Norman dishes
such as baked pigeon and *tartare de
langoustine* (langoustine tartare).

### ② Gourmandises, Cormeilles
MAP F3 ▪ 29 rue de l'Abbaye ▪ 02 32 20
63 42 ▪ Closed Wed dinner, Mon, Tue ▪ €€

This former cheese shop is the best
restaurant in Cormeilles, serving a
short menu of hearty dishes such as
*pot-au-feu* (beef stew) and baked cod.

### ③ Auberge des Deux Tonneaux, Pierrefitte-en-Auge
MAP E3 ▪ Le Bourg ▪ 02 31 64 09 31
▪ Closed Mon dinner, Tue (exc Jul &
Aug) ▪ No disabled access ▪ €

Gorgeous views and traditional
country fare such as suckling pig can
be enjoyed at this 17th-century inn.

### ④ Au P'tit Normand, Cambremer-en-Auge
MAP E4 ▪ Pl de l'Église ▪ 02 31 32
03 20 ▪ Closed Sun dinner, Mon, Jan–
mid-Feb ▪ €

This snug bistro is a local favourite
for home-made terrines, mixed
salads and Norman classics.

### ⑤ Belle Île-sur-Risle, Pont-Audemer
MAP F3 ▪ 112 rte de Rouen ▪ 02 32
56 96 22 ▪ Closed mid-Nov–mid-Mar
▪ €€

A romantic private island provides the
setting for this elegant mansion hotel
and restaurant. The *pastilla de lapin*
(rabbit in filo pastry) is wonderful.

### ⑥ Les Vapeurs, Trouville
MAP E3 ▪ 160–162 quai Fernand
Moureaux ▪ 02 31 88 15 24 ▪ €

Fabulous *moules frîtes*, desserts
with lashings of *crème fraîche*
and crisp white wines ensure this
place is always extremely busy.

Popular restaurant Les Vapeurs

### ⑦ Le Bréard, Honfleur
MAP F3 ▪ 7 rue du Puits ▪ 02 31
89 53 40 ▪ Closed Mon; Tue–Thu lunch
(Jul & Sep: open daily, dinner) ▪ €€€

This elegant restaurant specializes in
beautifully presented gourmet
dishes made from local ingredients.

### ⑧ Le Bistrot d'à Côté, Port-en-Bessin
MAP C3 ▪ 12 rue Michel Lefournier
▪ 02 31 51 79 12 ▪ Closed Sun–Mon
(Jul–Aug: Mon) ▪ €

The blue-and-white decor befits the
harbourside setting of this bistro.
The seafood is deliciously fresh.

### ⑨ La Ferme de la Haute Crémonville, St-Étienne-du-Vauvray
MAP H3 ▪ Rte de Crémonville ▪ 02 32 59 14
22 ▪ Closed Wed dinner, Sat lunch, Sun ▪ €

Set in a traditional farmhouse, this
place dishes up tasty local cuisine.

### ⑩ La Fine Fourchette, Falaise
MAP E4 ▪ 52 rue Georges
Clemenceau ▪ 02 31 90 08 59
▪ Closed 2 weeks Feb ▪ €€

Just outside Falaise, this place serves
Norman dishes with a refined twist.

*See map on pp92–3*

# 🔟 Northwestern Normand

Normandy's northwest is a world of its own. Thrusting into the English Channel is the Cotentin Peninsula, with picturesque little ports, long, unspoiled beaches, and gannets and shearwaters wheeling in the sky above wild and windblown headlands. Cotentin's proud maritime heritage is evident, especially in the important strategic port and naval base of Cherbourg, and it was from here in the Middle Ages that the descendants of Norse settlers set sail to establish kingdoms in Sicily and southern Italy. Further south, in the heart of the region – which encompasses the *département* of Manche – lies the marshy landscape of the Marais du Cotentin et du Bessin, a paradise for nature lovers. Further south, there are meadows and hedgerows *(bocage)*, and the lovely River Vire, seemingly made for pleasure.

**Painted carving at Coutances cathedral**

## AREA MAP OF NORTHWESTERN NORMANDY

| | |
|---|---|
| **1** | **Top 10 Sights** *see pp103–5* |
| ① | **Places to Eat** *see p109* |
| ① | **The Best of the Rest** *see p106* |
| ① | **Highlights of the Cotentin Coast** *see p107* |
| ① | **Family Outings** *see p108* |

Rosslare
Poole, Portsmouth
Barfleur
Cherbourg-Maupertus
La Hague Peninsula
Cherbourg
St-Vaast-la-Hougue
Flamanville
Les Pieux
N13
Valognes
Négreville
Utah Beach
Bricquebec
St-Sauveur-le-Vicomte
Barneville-Carteret
Portbail
Ste-Mère-Église
Omaha Beach
Parc Régional des Marais du Cotentin
Carentan
N13
Isigny-sur-Mer
Colleville-sur-Mer
Bayeux
Lessay
St-Jean-de-Daye
Tournières
Périers
Marchésieux
Tilly-sur-Seulles
Gouville-sur-Mer
Gratot
St-Lô
CALVADOS
Coutances
La Vacquerie
Pays de Bocage
Villers-Bocage
Montmartin-sur-Mer
Vallée de la Vire
La Ferrière-Harang
MANCHE
Trelly
Îles Chausey
Bréhal
Abbaye de Hambye
Percy
Campeaux
Le Bény-Bocage
Granville
Vire
Vassy
La Haye-Pesnel
Villedieu-les-Poêles

0 km 10
0 miles 10

*Previous pages Granville's upper town*

### 1 Utah Beach
**MAP B3**

On D-Day, 6 June 1944, the eastern coast of the Cotentin Peninsula, codenamed Utah Beach, received thousands of American troops, backed up by paratroopers that were dropped inland around Ste-Mère-Eglise (see pp34–7).

### 2 Cherbourg
**MAP B2 ■ Tourist office: 2 quai Alexandre III ■ 02 33 93 52 02**

There's more to Cherbourg than meets the eye, and of particular note is La Cité de la Mer, which is Europe's deepest aquarium (see p54). For a good view of the port, drive to the hilltop Fort du Roule, which houses the Musée de la Libération, recalling the events leading to Cherbourg's liberation on 27 June 1944. Most activity is centred on the market square, pl Général-de-Gaulle, and along shopping streets such as rue Tour-Carrée and rue de la Paix. The town's collection of fine art in the Musée Thomas-Henry (open mid-Mar–Dec) includes portraits by Jean-François Millet (see p48). Parc Emmanuel Liais has small botanical gardens and a densely packed Musée d'Histoire Naturelle.

### 3 La Hague Peninsula
**MAP A2 ■ Tourist office: 1 pl de la Madeleine, Beaumont-Hague ■ 02 33 52 74 94**

Calm and lovely on a sunny spring day, rugged and windswept during a winter storm, this furthest prong of Cotentin is stunningly beautiful. Its stone villages, majestic cliffs, jagged rocks and hidden coves are more reminiscent of Brittany than Normandy, and the presence of a vast nuclear power station in the middle does not detract – at least not too much – from the glorious coastline (see p105).

Lessay's compact abbey church

### 4 Lessay
**MAP B3 ■ Tourist office: 11 pl St-Cloud ■ 02 33 45 14 34**

The simple, comforting lines of Lessay's abbey church, St-Trinité, make it one of the most beautiful Romanesque buildings in Normandy. Dating from 1098, it was almost destroyed in 1944, but has been magnificently reconstructed using original materials. The interior is plain and lovely, with fine stained glass adding warmth. Sleepy Lessay's big moment comes in the second week of September, when thousands converge for the convivial three-day Foire de Sainte-Croix (see p81).

**The rugged Hague Peninsula**

### ⑤ Villedieu-les-Poêles
**MAP B5 ▪ Tourist office: 8 pl des Costils ▪ 02 33 61 05 69**

Since the 13th century, this little town has been the capital of copper – pots and pans are on sale everywhere. In the Atelier de Cuivre, you can see craftsmen at work, while the atmospheric Fonderie des Cloches gives an insight into the making of bells (clay, horse dung and goat hair are a few components). Another local craft, lacemaking, is covered in the Musée de la Dentellière.

### ⑥ Coutances
**MAP B4 ▪ Tourist office: pl Georges Leclerc ▪ 02 33 19 08 10**

This isolated corner of France is home to a great cathedral: a soaring stone rocket crowning the hill around which the town of Coutances clusters. In the 13th century, a new Norman Gothic cathedral was built on the remains of the previous, fire-damaged Romanesque one. Its remarkable octagonal lantern rises to 41 m (135 ft), and its many towers, spires and pointed arches sweep the eye skywards. In town, the flower-filled Jardin des Plantes makes a perfect setting for some of the concerts that take place during May's Jazz sous les Pommiers festival *(see p80)*.

**LE BOCAGE**

A rolling landscape of mixed woodland and meadow, bordered by banks topped with high, thick hedgerows, and bisected by narrow, sunken lanes – this is the *bocage* that covers much of Normandy, particularly around St-Lô and Vire. Pastoral in peacetime, it proved a nightmare for the Allies in 1944, making progress against the enemy near impossible.

**Abbaye de Hambye's roofless chancel**

### ⑦ Abbaye de Hambye
**MAP B4 ▪ Open Apr–Sep: 10am–noon, 2–6pm Wed–Mon (daily Jul–Aug) ▪ Adm charge**

Tucked beneath a wooded escarpment by the River Sienne, Hambye's roofless remains have an immediately calming effect on visitors. The restored monastic buildings of this 12th-century Benedictine abbey now host exhibitions and concerts.

### ⑧ Vallée de la Vire
**MAP C4 ▪ Tourist office: 60 rue de la Poterne ▪ 02 14 29 00 17**

As it winds towards the sea, the River Vire cuts through granite schists, forming a ribbon of water amid glorious countryside. Towpaths border most of the river between Vire and St-Lô, so you can picnic, cycle, walk or horse-ride alongside. Condé-sur-Vire is the place for canoeing, while at Roches de Ham, an 80-m (260-ft) rock face towers

**Notre-Dame cathedral, Coutances**

above the river, offering magnificent views of the valley. It is also home to a welcome crêperie and cider bar in summer. Nearby, the grand chapel at the village of La Chapelle-sur-Vire has been a place of pilgrimage since the 12th century. At Torigni-sur-Vire, the Château de Matignon houses a fine collection of tapestries.

### 9 Granville
MAP B5 ■ Tourist office: 4 cours Jonville ■ 02 33 91 30 03

At first sight, Granville seems an unlikely setting for one of Normandy's most popular seaside resorts (see p67). Ramparts enclose the upper town, which sits on a rocky spur overlooking the Baie du Mont-St-Michel. The town developed from the fortifications built by the English in 1439 as part of their assault on the Mont. In the gatehouse, the Musée de Vieux Granville recounts Granville's long seafaring tradition. The lower town is the resort, with a casino, promenades and public gardens. From the port, boat trips run to the Îles Chausey.

### 10 Parc Régional des Marais du Cotentin
MAP B3 ■ Espace de Découverte: Les Ponts d'Ouve, St-Côme-du-Mont ■ 02 33 71 65 30

The band of low-lying marshes and water meadows stretching across the base of the Cotentin Peninsula forms a regional park, with rich birdlife, plus houses made from clay and straw. Carentan is the gateway town, with a reception centre at Les Ponts d'Ouve on the D913, in the midst of a watery landscape. Visitors can explore on foot or by boat.

**Parc Régional des Marais du Cotentin**

---

## A DAY IN COTENTIN

### ▶ MORNING

Leave Cherbourg on the D901 toward **St-Pierre-Église**. After 15 km (9 miles), turn onto the D355 to pretty **Le Vast** in the heart of the lovely Val de Saire. Stop to buy a delicious *brioche du Vast* from Olivier Thebault, 12 les Moulins. Follow the river on the D25 to **Valcanville**, then on the D125 to **La Pernelle**, climbing the steep granite hill to the church and a magnificent panorama of the coast.

In **St-Vaast-la-Hougue** (see p106), book a table for lunch and sample the famous oysters at **France et des Fuchsias** (see p109), then stock up on food and wine at the family-run emporium **Gosselin**, trading since 1889. If there's time, take a trip to **Île de Tatihou**, just offshore (see p106).

### AFTERNOON

From St-Vaast, it's a quick drive along the D14 to **Quineville**, then the coastal D421 to **Utah Beach** to contemplate the events of June 1944 (see pp34–7). After a bracing walk along the beach and dunes, head inland to **Ste-Mère-Église** (see p106) and its church, perhaps pausing for refreshments at Café de la Libération in rue Général-de-Gaulle.

From Ste-Mère-Église, drive into the watery heart of the Cotentin marshlands, ending the day on the banks of the Douve at **Les Moitiers-en-Bauptois** at the delightful **Auberge de l'Ouve** (open Apr–Sep; 02 33 21 16 26), where local eels are the speciality.

*See map on p102* ←

# The Best of the Rest

### 1 Valognes
MAP B2 ■ Tourist office: pl du Château ■ 02 33 40 11 55

Though badly damaged in 1944, Valognes retains traces of its glory days as the "Versailles of the North", including the Hôtel de Beaumont, a splendid 18th-century mansion.

### 2 Portbail
MAP A3 ■ Tourist office: 26 rue Philippe Lebel ■ 02 33 04 03 07

A lovely village with access to two fine beaches. In summer, it hosts an excellent market every Tuesday.

### 3 Barneville-Carteret
MAP A3 ■ Tourist office: 15 rue Guillaume le Conquérant ■ 02 33 04 90 58

This lively resort comprises the villages of Barneville, Carteret and Barneville-Plage *(see p66)*. Its rocky headland, Cap de Carteret, makes for a bracing coastal walk.

### 4 St-Sauveur-le-Vicomte
MAP B3 ■ 02 33 21 50 44 ■ Open Apr–Oct: 2–6pm Mon, Wed–Fri & Sun ■ Adm charge

The 12th-century castle houses the Musée Barbey-d'Aurevilly, dedicated to the 19th-century novelist who was born in the town *(see p50)*.

### 5 St-Vaast-la-Hougue and Île de Tatihou
MAP B2 ■ Tourist office: 1 pl Général-de-Gaulle ■ 02 33 71 99 71

The harbour of this small port was fortified after the French defeat in 1692, as was the Île de Tatihou – now the site of a garden, bird-watching post and maritime museum.

### 6 Abbaye de Cérisy-la-Fôret
MAP C3 ■ Open Apr & Sep: Tue–Sun; May–Aug: daily; Oct: pm Sat & Sun ■ Adm charge

This Benedictine abbey was founded in 1032 by Duke Robert the Magnificent. The ruins of the huge nave recall the monastery's former importance.

### 7 St-Lô
MAP C4 ■ Tourist office: 60 rue de la Poterne ■ 02 14 29 00 17

The regional capital suffered severe war damage, as testified by its many memorials and striking half-restored cathedral. The Musée des Beaux-Arts displays some great works of art.

### 8 Château de Gratot
MAP B4 ■ 02 33 45 18 49 ■ Open daily ■ Adm charge

The roofless remains of this once-great château lie in quiet countryside. An exhibition tells its story.

### 9 Ste-Mère-Église
MAP B3 ■ Tourist office: rue Eisenhower ■ 02 33 21 00 33

The church here was made famous by the film *The Longest Day*. The Ferme Musée du Cotentin gives an insight into early 1900s rural life. There is also a World War II museum.

### 10 Château de Pirou
MAP B4 ■ Open mid-Mar–Sep, mid-Oct–mid-Nov: Wed–Mon ■ Adm charge

Set on an island in the middle of an artificial lake, this remote 12th-century fortress is a stirring sight.

Île de Tatihou

# Highlights of the Cotentin Coast

**Wild Val de Saire coastline**

## 1 Val de Saire
MAP B2

The gentle, verdant valley east of Barfleur is in sharp contrast to the wild coastline (see p71).

## 2 Querqueville
MAP A2

Beside the hilltop church, and surrounded by a cemetery packed with ornate marble tombs, stands 10th-century St-Germain, the oldest chapel in western France.

## 3 Château de Nacqueville
MAP A2 ■ Open May–Sep: noon–5pm Thu, Fri, Sun & public hols ■ Adm charge

The park of this 16th-century château, with its romantic turreted gatehouse, is loveliest in May and June when the rhododendrons are in bloom.

## 4 Gruchy
MAP A2

This tiny seaside village includes the humble birthplace of Jean-François Millet (see p48), open to the public in summer. Walk to the dramatic Rocher du Castel-Vendon; Millet's painting of it can be seen in the Musée Thomas-Henry in Cherbourg (see p103).

## 5 Port Racine
MAP A2

En route to Cap de la Hague, France's smallest port is tucked beneath the road. From here, follow signs to Jardins Prévert, an oasis at the head of a wild valley.

## 6 Îles Chausey
MAP A4

This is a collection of tiny islands and islets in the Channel. The largest, Grande Île, has sweeping sandy beaches and just one hotel. In summer it attracts day-trippers from Granville, an hour's boat ride away.

## 7 Omonville-la-Petite
MAP A2

The churchyard here contains the uncarved headstone of poet Jacques Prévert, and the graves of his wife and daughter. Nearby is his house (see p51).

## 8 Barfleur
MAP B2

It is said that William the Conqueror's invasion vessel was built in this fishing port (see p56). Its lighthouse, at Gatteville, is one of the tallest in France, with 365 steps; the reward for climbing up it is a fine panorama.

**Boats moored in low tide at Barfleur**

## 9 Vauville
MAP A2

The twin attractions here are the subtropical gardens of Château de Vauville and a fine beach that is perfect for sand yachting (see p68).

## 10 Nez de Jobourg
MAP A2

The desolate Baie d'Ecalgrain sweeps round to this impressive promontory. From here, the road to Vauville is dominated by the Usine Atomique de la Hague nuclear power station.

See map on p102

# Family Outings

### ① L'Attelage des Grandes Marées, Gouville-sur-Mer

MAP B4 ▪ Booking essential: tourist office, 1 rue du Nord, 02 33 47 84 33

You can visit this oyster park at low tide in a horse-drawn carriage.

L'Attelage des Grandes Marées

### ② La Cité de la Mer, Cherbourg

Man's conquest of the deep is the theme of Cherbourg's former Gare Maritime Transatlantique (no children under 6) *(see p54)*.

### ③ Mini-trains

Train du Cotentin: MAP A3; 02 33 04 70 08 ▪ Mini-train des Marais: MAP C3–B3; 02 33 07 91 77

Take a ride on a mini-train. One runs along the coast from Carteret to Portbail, the other through marshland from St-Lô to Periers.

### ④ Manoir de Dur-Ecu

MAP A2 ▪ Open Jul–Sep: 11am–1pm, 3–7pm Tue–Thu ▪ Adm charge

This lovely ancestral manor house (not itself open to visitors) hides in its grounds a delightful surprise: a maize maze, designed by Adrian Fisher.

### ⑤ Water Sports

Jolie France: 02 33 50 31 81; vedettejoliefrance.com ▪ Cherbourg: cotentin-nautisme.fr

The *Jolie France* sails from Granville to Chausey's Grand Île *(see p107)*. Cherbourg offers a range of activities, from kayaking to pleasure cruises.

### ⑥ Île de Tatihou

Children enjoy the amphibious craft that crosses to this tiny pleasure island with a fascinating history. It is just off St-Vaast-la-Hougue *(see p106)*.

### ⑦ Musée du Bocage Normand

MAP C4 ▪ Bd de la Commune, St-Lô ▪ 02 33 56 26 98 ▪ Open Apr–Sep: 1:30–6:30pm Tue–Sun; Oct: 2–6pm Tue–Sun ▪ Adm charge

An absorbing museum located in old farm buildings. It shows how the region was farmed in centuries gone by, with plenty of interactive exhibits and reconstructions.

### ⑧ Ferme aux 5 Saisons, Flamanville

MAP A2 ▪ 02 33 04 56 84 ▪ Open Jul & Aug: pm Mon–Fri ▪ Adm charge

A farm for children: see an apple press in action, visit the animals and bake bread for tea.

### ⑨ Vélorail, Vallée de la Vire

MAP C4 ▪ Condé-sur-Vire ▪ 02 33 05 46 55 ▪ velorail-normandie.fr ▪ Open Jul & Aug: daily; mid-Apr–Jun & Sep: Sat, Sun, public hols

Ride the area's disused railways in a pedal-powered buggy.

### ⑩ Musée Christian Dior

MAP B5 ▪ Les Rhumbs, Granville ▪ 02 33 61 48 21 ▪ Open mid-May–Sep: daily ▪ Adm charge

This exhibition of designs by Dior and other top couturiers is set in his picturesque childhood home.

Musée Christian Dior

# Places to Eat

## 1 Le Faitout, Cherbourg
MAP B2 ▪ 25 Tour Carrée ▪ 02
33 04 25 04 ▪ Closed Sun ▪ €

This bistro is a bastion of culinary
tradition. Locals flock here for the
excellent fixed-price menus that
feature wholesome dishes such as
sea bass with vegetable risotto or
fillet of beef with Camembert sauce.

## 2 Le Moulin à Vent, St-Germain-des-Vaux
MAP A2 ▪ Hameau Danneville ▪ 02 33
52 75 20 ▪ Closed Wed & Thu except
Jul–Aug ▪ €

Enjoy glorious views and very fresh
seafood at very reasonable prices.

## 3 Le Marine, Barneville-Carteret
MAP A3 ▪ 11 rue de Paris ▪ 02 33 53
83 31 ▪ Closed Mon lunch, Thu
dinner, Sun dinner ▪ €€

The dishes at this hotel restaurant
with harbour views range from French
classics such as pork rib with black
pudding sauce to the more modern
such as red mullet in a parmesan
crust with an onion compôte.

## 4 Ferme de Malte, Villedieu-les-Poêles
MAP B5 ▪ 11 rue Tétrel ▪ 02 33 91 35 91
▪ Closed Wed & Sun dinner, Mon ▪ €€

Owned by the Knights of Malta, who
have a long connection with the town,
this smart restaurant specializes in
fish, and has two dining rooms.

## 5 La Ferme des Mares, Saint-Germain-sur-Ay
MAP B3 ▪ 02 33 17 01 02 ▪ Closed
Wed, Sun dinner ▪ €

This restaurant, once a fortified
Norman farm, serves the best local
fish, lamb and traditional cheeses.

## 6 Auberge de Goury, Auderville
MAP A2 ▪ Porte de Goury ▪ 02 33 52 77
01 ▪ Closed Sun dinner, Mon, Jan ▪ €€

At the very end of Cap de la Hague,
this restaurant serves *fruits de mer*
(seafood platter), and fresh fish and
meats grilled over an open fire.

## 7 La Plancha, Agon-Coutainville
MAP B4 ▪ 77 rue Dramard ▪ 02 33 47
26 77 ▪ Closed Tue & Wed (Sep–Jun) ▪ €

This trendy beach brasserie has
fabulous sea views and an original
menu of fresh seafood and fish
platters, plus tapas.

## 8 France et des Fuchsias, St-Vaast-la-Hougue
MAP B2 ▪ 20 rue Maréchal Foch ▪ 02 33
54 40 41 ▪ Closed Mon; Tue lunch ▪ €€

The oysters are a highlight at this
superb seafood restaurant.

France et des Fuchsias seafood

## 9 Verte Campagne, Trelly
MAP B4 ▪ 02 33 47 65 33
▪ Closed Wed ▪ €

A wide enough range of menus to
suit most pockets is available at this
elegant restaurant in a rustic, ivy-
covered farmhouse (see p130).

## 10 L'Auberge, Mesnil-Rogues
MAP B4 ▪ 02 33 61 37 12 ▪ Closed Tue
dinner, Wed dinner, Sun dinner, Mon ▪ €

Hams and legs of lamb are spit-
roasted at this cosy *auberge*. The
fish dishes are also excellent.

*See map on p102*

# TOP 10 Southern Normandy

From the astonishing sight of Mont-St-Michel, appearing like a fabulous mirage out of the pancake-flat landscape that surrounds it, to the equine elegance of the national stud at Haras du Pin or the human charm of romantic Château d'O, this region, which consists of the *département* of Orne and the southern part of Manche, is crammed with history and variety. The scenery is just as varied: there's the rugged beauty of the Pays d'Alençon in the Parc Régional de Normandie-Maine, where bands of thick forest cover the high ridges; the wooded Mortainais, with its steep valleys and exhilarating waterfalls; the gently rolling pastureland of La Perche, interrupted by cool, deep forests; the narrow lanes and pretty, flower-filled villages of the Pays du Bocage Ornais; and the flat salt marshes of the Baie de Mont-St-Michel.

**Mont-St-Michel manuscript, Scriptorial d'Avranches**

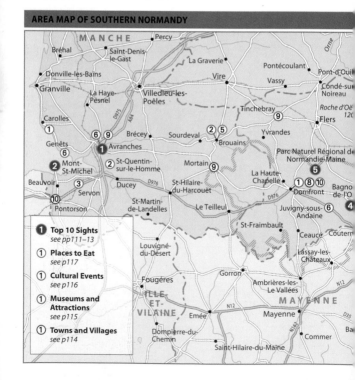

AREA MAP OF SOUTHERN NORMANDY

1 **Top 10 Sights**
see pp111–13

1 **Places to Eat**
see p117

1 **Cultural Events**
see p116

1 **Museums and Attractions**
see p115

1 **Towns and Villages**
see p114

### 1 Avranches

**MAP B5** ■ **Tourist office: 2 rue du Général de Gaulle** ■ **02 33 58 00 22**

Avranches has a long and historic association with Mont-St-Michel (see pp12–15), which it overlooks across the bay (one of the best views is from the Jardin des Plantes). St Aubert, who

**St Aubert's skull, Avranches**

founded the abbey there, was Bishop of Avranches; his skull, complete with the hole made by St Michael's finger, is on display in the Basilique de St-Gervais et St-Protais. In an annexe of the former episcopal palace, the Musée d'Avranches contains wonderful collections of medieval sculpture and religious art, and in the Scriptorial d'Avranches you can see the Mont-St-Michel manuscripts, dating back to the 8th century.

### 2 Mont-St-Michel

Despite being the most photographed sight in France, the ethereal beauty of this vast abbey can still take your breath away (see pp12–15).

### 3 Alençon

**MAP E6** ■ **Tourist office: Maison d'Ozé, pl de la Magdelaine** ■ **02 33 80 66 33**

This handsome town was a famous lacemaking centre in the 17th and 18th centuries. Examples are displayed in the Musée des Beaux-Arts et de la Dentelle, which presents a history of the industry alongside paintings and Cambodian artifacts. The intricate stonework on the façade of the Église de Notre-Dame even resembles lace; inside, there's a chapel to Alençon-born St Thérèse.

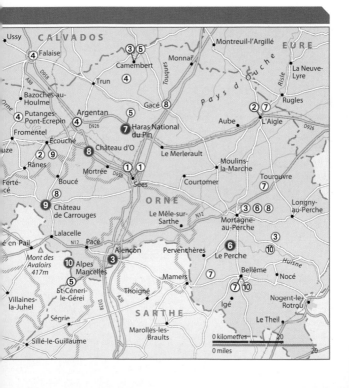

### 4 Bagnoles-de-l'Orne
MAP D5 ■ Tourist office: pl du Marché ■ 02 33 37 85 66

Clamber to the top of the Roc au Chien for a panorama of this refined spa town steeped in legend *(see p66)*. Its lake, casino, park and avenues of chic houses were built for the wealthy who came to take the waters in the late 19th century. Ailing visitors still flock to the Établissement Thermal, in its striking *belle époque* building.

### 5 Parc Naturel Régional de Normandie-Maine
MAP D5–E5 ■ Maison du Parc: Carrouges ■ 02 33 81 13 33 ■ Open Apr–Jun & Sep–mid Oct: 10am–noon & 2–6pm daily; Jul–Aug: 10am–12:30pm & 2–6:30pm daily

With a landscape marked by escarpments and forests in the *haut pays* of the Alpes Mancelles, and by rolling hills, *bocage* and open country in the *bas pays* at Saosnois and around Alençon and Sées, this vast natural park dips south to the Pays-de-Loire. Pick up maps and itineraries at the Maison du Parc in Carrouges. Nature centres are scattered through the park *(see p60)*.

### 6 Le Perche
MAP G6–H6 ■ Tourist office: 88 rue St-Blaise, Alençon ■ 02 33 28 07 00

Still relatively unknown, this area is famous for its powerful Percheron horses and its manors. Perche manors are quite different from typical half-timbered Norman farmhouses; they are defensive buildings, made of stone and embellished with turrets and towers. The surrounding countryside is gentle, with undulating hills, dense forest and lush valleys. Grazing Percherons (draughthorses from the region) add an air of serenity.

**The stately Haras National du Pin**

**NORMANDY HORSES**

In stud farms throughout Orne, Manche and Calvados, horses of the highest calibre are bred, raised and trained for competition. The four main breeds are thoroughbreds – spirited, highly strung racehorses; Norman trotters, a mixed breed with a longer career; cobs – sturdy carriage horses; and Percherons, ideal for heavy farm work.

**Le Perche's Manoir de Courboyer**

Chief among Perche's seductive villages and small towns are Mortagne and Bellême *(see p114)*.

### 7 Haras National du Pin
MAP E5 ■ Le Pin-au-Haras ■ 02 33 36 68 68 ■ www.haras-national-du-pin.com ■ Open Apr–Sep: 10am–6pm daily; Mar, Oct: pm Sat & Sun ■ Tours every half hour ■ Adm charge

You don't have to be a horse lover to be impressed by the style and splendour of the national stud, a "Versailles for horses" founded by Colbert in the mid-17th century with the approval of the Sun King himself. Colbert commissioned Pierre Le Mousseux to design it. At the end of a long, grassy ride through the surrounding woods, the main château and two elegant former stable blocks enclose a horseshoe-shaped courtyard (Colbert's Court), scene of horse and carriage displays on Thursday afternoons in summer. Tours visit the forge, tack room and stables, where some 100 stallions are kept at stud.

### 8 Château d'O

MAP E5 ▪ Mortrée ▪ Opening times vary: phone Argentan tourist office for details, 02 33 67 12 48 (1 Aug–9 Sep: 02 33 12 67 46)

With fairy-tale turrets and steep roofs reflected in the limpid, green waters of its moat, this early Renaissance château is utterly enchanting. It was largely built during the 15th and 16th centuries, with a west wing – now the living quarters – added in the 18th. You can wander in the grounds or take a tour of the interior, furnished in mainly 18th-century style.

Château d'O, Mortrée

### 9 Château de Carrouges

MAP E6 ▪ 02 33 27 20 32 ▪ Open Apr–mid-Jun, Sep: 10am–noon & 2–6pm; mid-Jun–Aug: 9:30am–noon & 2–6:30pm; Oct–Mar: 10am–noon & 2–5pm ▪ Adm charge

Until it was bought by the state in 1936, this imposing château had been in the Le Veneur de Tillières family for almost 500 years. Founded by Jean de Carrouges in the 14th century, it has all the attributes of a grand château: moats, terraces, gardens, and an elegant 16th-century gatehouse (see p116).

### 10 Alpes Mancelles

MAP E6 ▪ Tourist office: 19 av du Docteur Riant, Fresnay-sur-Sarthe; 02 43 33 28 04; Closed Mon

In the Parc Naturel Régional de Normandie-Maine, on Normandy's southern border, is this rugged landscape of valleys and forests. Mont des Avaloirs, at 417 m (1,368 ft), is the joint highest peak in western France. Of the area's lovely villages, the jewel is St-Céneri-le-Gérei (see p114).

▶ **MORNING**

Pick up a "Circuit du Patrimoine" from the tourist office in the old market in **Mortagne-au-Perche** (pl du Général-de-Gaulle), and walk its route (see p114), popping into the Église de Notre-Dame to see the glorious altarpiece. Finish with a coffee in the **Hôtel Tribunal** (see p117).

Leave Mortagne-au-Perche on the D931 towards Mamers. Turn left on the D275 and follow signs to **La Perrière**, an enchanting village of colourful cottages and tempting *brocantes* (antiques shops), with a glorious view. Take the RF225 through the peaceful **Forêt de Bellême** (see p62) as far as the D931. Turn right for **Bellême** (see p114). Go through the town and turn right onto the D203 to Nocé, where the **Auberge des Trois J** (1 pl Docteur-Gireaux) is an excellent lunch stop.

**AFTERNOON**

Leave Nocé on the D9 and stop off at the handsome turreted **Manoir de Courboyer**, housing the Maison du Parc de Perche. You can visit the manor and explore the extensive grounds, which harbour orchards, ponds, horses and donkeys. Regular exhibitions and workshops are held here. Head back onto the D9, then turn right onto the D5 to the impressive **Chapelle-Montligeon**, a huge basilica built in the early 1900s. After a look around, and perhaps a detour to the lovely **Forêt de Réno-Valdieu** (see p62), head to the welcoming **Le Montligeon** restaurant (14 rue Principale) for dinner.

*See map on pp110–11* ←

# Towns and Villages

**1 Sées**
MAP E5 ▪ Tourist office: pl du Général-de-Gaulle ▪ 02 33 28 74 79
A bishopric since the 4th century, Sées has a few religious buildings: a Gothic cathedral with a very fine interior, a former Bishop's Palace and an abbey.

**2 L'Aigle**
MAP F5 ▪ Tourist office: pl Fulbert de Beina ▪ 02 33 24 12 40
Traditionally a metalworking area, the town plays host each Tuesday to Normandy's biggest market (see p77). St Martin's church and the château are both worth a visit.

**3 Camembert**
MAP E4 ▪ La Ferme "Maison de Camembert": 02 33 12 10 37; open May–Sep, Apr & Oct: Wed–Sun; adm charge
Popularized by Napoleon III, the famous cheese was first made here by Marie Harel around 1790. Some farms still use her original method.

**4 Argentan**
MAP E5 ▪ Tourist office: pl du Marché ▪ 02 33 67 12 48
Apart from its role at the end of the Battle of Normandy, commemorated by the nearby memorial, the town is known for lace and for horse racing.

**5 St-Céneri-le-Gérei**
MAP E6
Officially listed as one of France's top 100 prettiest, this small stone village above the River Sarthe has inspired generations of artists (see p57).

**6 Mortagne-au-Perche**
MAP F6 ▪ Tourist office: pl de Gaulle ▪ 02 33 83 34 37
Sometime regional capital, and an excellent base for exploring, this bustling, historic hilltop town is famous for its black pudding.

**7 Bellême**
MAP F6 ▪ Tourist office: bd Bansard des Bois ▪ 02 33 73 09 69
On a rocky spur overlooking forest, ruined fortifications nestle among well-preserved 17th- and 18th-century houses. There's a mushroom fair in late September.

**8 Domfront**
MAP D5 ▪ Tourist office: pl de la Roirie ▪ 02 33 38 53 97
Perched above the Varenne Gorge, Domfront affords open views over the pear orchards of the Bocage Passais. The ramparts and castle are evidence of the town's turbulent history.

**9 Mortain**
MAP C5 ▪ Tourist office: rue du Bourg Lopin ▪ 02 33 59 19 74
Mortain is surrounded by woods, granite and waterfalls. The Grande and Petite cascades are within easy walking distance of the town centre.

**10 Pontorson**
MAP B5 ▪ Tourist office: pl de l'Hôtel de Ville ▪ 02 33 60 20 65
Pontorson is something of a gateway to Mont-St-Michel. Its 12th-century church is a fine example of Norman Romanesque architecture.

St-Céneri-le-Gérai

# Museums and Attractions

Interior of the Église St-Julien

## 1 Église St-Julien, Domfront

MAP D5 ▪ Pl du Commerce ▪ Interior closed for renovations
Built of concrete in 1926, this church boasts Neo-Byzantine-style mosaics.

## 2 Ecomusée du Moulin de la Sée, Brouains

MAP C5 ▪ 2 le Moulin de Brouains ▪ 02 33 49 76 64 ▪ Open Apr–Jun & Sep–Oct: pm Wed–Sat; Jul–Aug: Tue–Fri, pm Sat & Sun ▪ Adm charge
Admire the giant waterwheel that drove the machinery of this former paper mill on the River Sée.

## 3 Jardins de Pongirard

MAP G6 ▪ Monceaux-au-Perche ▪ 02 33 73 61 49 ▪ Open May–Sep 10am–6pm Thu–Tue
Manoir du Pongirard's glorious gardens feature lavender, an ancient lime tree and 30 kinds of euphorbia.

## 4 Fromagerie Durand

MAP E5 ▪ Ferme de la Hérronière ▪ 02 33 39 08 08 ▪ Open 10am–12:30pm, 3–5:30pm Mon–Sat ▪ Adm charge
Visit one of the last fromageries to make Camembert in the traditional way, using unpasteurized milk.

## 5 La Maison du Camembert, Camembert

MAP F4 ▪ Le Bourg ▪ 02 33 12 10 37 ▪ Open May–Sep: daily; Apr & Oct: Wed–Sun ▪ Adm charge
Dedicated to the famous cheese, this museum features a reconstruction of an old production plant.

## 6 La Ferme du Cheval de Trait, Juvigny-sous-Andaine

MAP D5 ▪ La Michaudière ▪ 02 33 38 27 78 ▪ Jul–Aug: Wed, Thu, Sat & Sun (phone for times) ▪ Adm charge
See horse-drawn agricultural equipment, a miniature farm and displays by Percheron draughthorses.

## 7 Musée de l'Emmigration Percheronne au Canada, Tourouvre

MAP F5 ▪ 15 rue Mondrel ▪ 02 33 25 55 55 ▪ Open Apr–Oct: 10am–12:30pm, 2–6pm Tue–Sun ▪ Adm charge
A replica of the room where, in the 17th-century, locals signed emigration contracts for Quebec.

## 8 Musée de la Dame aux Camélias, Gacé

MAP F5 ▪ Château de Gacé ▪ 02 33 67 08 59 ▪ Open mid-Jun–mid-Sep: 2–6pm Tue–Sat ▪ Adm charge
This museum evokes the extravagant lifestyle of the heroine of Alexandre Dumas' famous novel, set in the Orne.

Musée de la Dame aux Camélias

## 9 Musée et Prison Royale, Tinchebray

MAP D5 ▪ 32 Grande Rue ▪ 02 33 64 23 55 ▪ Open Jul–Aug: 2:30–6pm Mon, Tue, Thu, Fri ▪ Adm charge
A chilling place, with a court room, cells and an ethnographic museum.

## 10 Attelage dans la Nature

MAP E4 ▪ L'Absoudière, Corbon ▪ 02 33 83 91 40 ▪ Apr–Sep
Travel the Percheron countryside along forest tracks and lanes in a traditional horse-drawn carriage.

*See map on pp110–11* ←

# Cultural Events

### 1 Les Musilumières de Sées

MAP E5 ■ Sées tourist office: 02 33 28 74 79 ■ Jul–mid-Sep: Fri–Sat

The latest technology is used in this sound-and-light show at Sées's 13th-century Gothic cathedral *(see p114)*.

**Lighting effects, Sées cathedral**

### 2 Septembre Musical de l'Orne

02 33 26 99 99 ■ www.septembre-musical.com ■ Sep: Fri–Sun

Churches, abbeys and châteaux provide settings for opera, chamber music, jazz and dance events.

### 3 Les Musicales de Mortagne

MAP F6 ■ Mortagne tourist office: 02 33 85 11 18 ■ late Jun–mid-Jul

Six chamber concerts by world-class performers are staged in stunning settings in Mortagne-au-Perche.

### 4 Les Hivernales, Falaise

MAP E4 ■ www.falaise-tourisme.com ■ early Dec–early Jan

The birthplace of William the Conqueror celebrates Christmas with lights, a craft market, choirs and medieval-themed events.

### 5 Les Jeudis du Pin, Le Pin-au-Haras

Jun–Sep: 3–4pm Thu

During the summer months, enjoy the weekly musical presentation of stallions, mares, foals and Norman donkeys at the prestigious national stud farm *(see p112)*.

### 6 Les Estivales d'Avranches

MAP B5 ■ Avranches tourist office: 02 33 58 00 22 ■ mid-Jul

This summer music festival stages concerts by established performers.

### 7 Le Marché d'Art, La Perrière

MAP F6 ■ Whit Sun & Mon

Dealers and connoisseurs flock to this village, which becomes a gallery for unknown and established artists.

### 8 Autour d'un Piano, Château de Carrouges

MAP E6 ■ Office Départemental de la Culture: 02 33 31 25 42 ■ www.ornetourisme.com ■ late Jul–Aug

This fine château makes a great venue for recitals by famous soloists and chamber ensembles.

### 9 Festival d'Art Actuel, Château de Serans, Écouché

MAP E5 ■ 61150 Écouché ■ 02 33 36 69 42 ■ late May–Sep

A contemporary art and crafts festival is held at a château near Argentan.

### 10 Les Médiévales de Domfront

MAP D5 ■ Maison des Associations: 02 33 38 56 66 ■ www.domfront-medievales.com ■ Aug

In odd-numbered years, actors and musicians re-create a medieval festival, with games and a market.

**Les Médiévales de Domfront**

# Places to Eat

**PRICE CATEGORIES**

For a three-course meal for one with half a bottle of wine (or equivalent meal), taxes and extra charges.

€ under €40   €€ €40–€60   €€€ over €60

**① La Grange de Tom, Champeaux**

MAP B5 ▪ 40 rte des Falaises ▪ 02 33 61 85 52 ▪ €

Set on the cliffs at Champeaux, this lovely former farm offers an irresistible view across the bay to Mont-St-Michel. The food, much of it grilled over an open fire, is a mix of traditional and modern.

**② Le Gué du Holme, St-Quentin-sur-le-Homme**

MAP B5 ▪ 14 rue des Estuaires ▪ 02 33 60 63 76 ▪ Closed Mon, Sat lunch, Sun dinner ▪ €€

A range of fresh fish, local farm produce and game are among the choices at this restaurant (see p130).

**③ Auberge du Terroir, Servon**

MAP B5 ▪ Le Bourg ▪ 02 33 60 17 92 ▪ Closed Wed, Sat lunch ▪ €

Located in a small village close to Mont-St-Michel, this friendly, good-value restaurant with rooms serves dishes made from local ingredients.

**④ Lion Verd, Putanges-Pont-Ecrepin**

MAP E5 ▪ 02 33 35 01 86 ▪ €

This local favourite has a pretty riverside terrace by a bridge over the Orne. Vegetarian dishes are always on the menu.

**⑤ Auberge du Moulin, Brouains**

MAP C5 ▪ 4 le Moulin de Brouains ▪ 02 33 59 50 60 ▪ Closed Sun dinner, Mon, Tue ▪ €

Diners can enjoy traditional, refined, home-made cuisine and excellent service in this former industrial mill.

**⑥ Chez François, Genêts**

MAP B5 ▪ Prés de la Mairie ▪ 02 33 70 83 98 ▪ Closed Wed, Thu ▪ €

This cave-like bistro on the Bay of Mont-St-Michel is known for its grilled meats and delicious desserts. Vegetarian options are very limited.

**⑦ Hôtel du Dauphin, L'Aigle**

MAP F5 ▪ pl de la Halle ▪ 02 33 84 18 00 ▪ Restaurant closed Sun dinner (brasserie open daily) ▪ €

The food at this comfortable, family-run hotel is excellent. Visitors can choose between the restaurant and brasserie.

**⑧ Tribunal, Mortagne-au-Perche**

MAP F6 ▪ 4 pl du Palais ▪ 02 33 25 04 77 ▪ €

A choice of classic and regional dishes is offered at this old, well-appointed inn on a quiet square (see p128).

Tribunal, Mortagne-au-Perche

**⑨ Le Tripot, Avranches**

MAP B5 ▪ 11 rue du Tripot ▪ 02 33 60 59 23 ▪ €

French dishes fused with world flavours are served at this bright, fashionable bistro.

**⑩ Le Relais St Louis, Bellême**

MAP F6 ▪ 1 bd Bonsard des Bois ▪ 02 33 73 12 21 ▪ Closed Sun dinner, Mon ▪ €€

This charming old coaching inn offers a reasonably priced daily menu, with dishes such as chicken cooked in cider or black pudding with potatoes braised in pommeau.

*See map on pp110–11*

# Streetsmart

**Brightly coloured Camembert labels**

# Getting To and Around Normandy

### Arriving by Air

With few international flights to Normandy, most air travellers fly to Paris and take a train. **Ryanair** flies from Dublin and to Dinard from East Midlands and Stansted; from the UK, **easyJet** flies to Paris Charles de Gaulle; **CityJet** flies to Paris Orly; **Flybe** flies from UK regional airports to Paris and Caen; and **HOP!** flies from Lyon to Caen.

### Arriving by Eurotunnel

Taking your car on the **Eurotunnel** shuttle from Folkestone to Calais takes around 35 minutes. The A16 motorway links Calais to Normandy, and the drive to Rouen takes 2 hours, or 3 hours to Caen.

### Arriving by Eurostar

**Eurostar** trains from London St Pancras International take 2 hours 20 minutes to reach Paris Gare du Nord. Travellers heading for Normandy can change at Lille – 1 hour 20 minutes from London – for connections to towns such as Rouen and Bayeux. Tickets can be bought directly from the Eurostar website.

### Arriving by Ferry

There are regular sailings from several UK ports across to Normandy.
**Brittany Ferries** sails to Cherbourg from both Portsmouth and Poole.

Portsmouth to Cherbourg takes 3 hours, while Poole–Cherbourg is 4 hours 15 minutes. There are also crossings from Portsmouth to Le Havre (5 hours, 30 minutes day crossing and 10 hours night crossing), from Plymouth to Roscoff (6–8 hours) and also a Portsmouth–Caen route (6–8 hours). You can step off the ferry in the fishing port of Ouistreham, a short drive from Caen.

**Transmanche Ferries** has two sailings per day to Dieppe from Newhaven, which takes about 4 hours.

Motorists are advised to book ahead, especially in high season. Foot passengers and cyclists can normally just turn up and board. Prices vary enormously depending on the season and how far in advance you book. You can compare prices and find cut-price fares using the **Ferry Savers** website.

### Arriving by River

The most romantic way to arrive in Normandy is from Paris by river. Two companies organize a seven-night Seine cruise from Paris to Rouen, which stops at Vernon, Les Andelys and Conflan: **Viking River Cruises** and **CrosiEurope**. Their itineraries differ, but one of the CroisiEurope routes includes stops at Giverny, Rouen and Honfleur.

### Travelling by Train

The excellent national rail network, **SNCF**, links the region's major towns and cities. Fares are quite reasonable. For the ultra-fast TGVs *(Trains à Grande Vitesse)* you'll need to pay a supplement at peak times. The slowest trains, marked TER on the time-tables, stop at all stations. Validate your ticket ("Compostez votre billet") in the machine at the station platform. Failure to do so is an offence.

### Travelling by Car

With your own car, you can venture off the beaten track. All the major rental companies operate in Normandy from airports, railway stations and city centres. Most require drivers to be over 21, with a clean licence. Before booking, look into fly-drive packages, which can be excellent value.

Depending on the type of road, four speed limits apply: on autoroutes, the limit is 130 kph (81 mph); on N or RN roads – dual carriageways – it's 110 kph (68 mph); on local D and minor C and V roads, it's 90 kph (56 mph); lastly, there's a limit of 50 kph (31 mph) in built-up areas.

By French law, you must carry ID, a driving licence, and car ownership and insurance details (you should take out emergency breakdown cover). You must add headlight beam deflectors to a right-hand drive car, and you should carry a red warning triangle, fire extinguisher, first-aid kit and a yellow reflective jacket.

If your car breaks down, wear your yellow reflective jacket and – walking behind the barrier for safety – place the red warning triangle 50–100 m (160–300 ft) behind it. If you have an accident, call the emergency services. *Postes d'appel d'urgence* (emergency telephones) are posted at 2-km (1.5-mile) intervals on autoroutes, 4 km (2.5 miles) on dual carriageways; they will connect you with rescue services via the traffic police (for a list of emergency phone numbers, see p123).

## Travelling by Bus

Bus routes link many of the region's major destinations, although schedules are geared to students and commuters rather than tourists, so there's a reduced service at weekends. Coastal routes tend to be the most reliable. Different companies run the network for each *département*; tourist offices have the details. A national bus service, **isilines**, runs a service between Rennes and Caen.

## City Transport

With the exception of central Rouen's fiendish one-way system, most cities are car-friendly, with plenty of pay-and-display parking and car parks. Public transport is largely reliable, with bus services in all towns and cities. Rouen has a tram system and a metro, and Caen has a tram system.

## Taxis

Taxis can only be picked up from taxi ranks *(stations de taxi)* or summoned by phone – not hailed on the street. Check your taxi has a meter before entering. Fares can vary from one *département* to another.

## Cycling

With its varied terrain and plentiful backroads, Normandy is a wonderful region for cycling. You can transport your bike by air, rail or ferry, or hire one in most towns and at some railway stations. If you're after a mountain bike, look out for the VTT sign *(vélos tout terrain)*. There are cycle paths throughout the region; tourist offices and local cycling associations have details.

If you're feeling adventurous, you could cycle all the way from Paris to Mont-St-Michel on the **Veloscenic**, a long-distance cycle path that takes in some of Normandy's loveliest countryside – or opt to cycle just a section of it.

## On Foot

Normandy is crisscrossed by hundreds of footpaths graded to suit walkers of all levels. The well-known *grande randonnée* (GR) trails, marked by red and white stripes, take walkers through some spectacular scenery. Regional tourist offices provide details and maps of all the GR routes in their *département*.

Tourist offices in larger towns publish a "Circuit du Patrimoine", a city tour that takes in all the sights.

## DIRECTORY

### AIRLINES

**CityJet**
w cityjet.com

**easyJet**
w easyjet.com

**Flybe**
w flybe.com

**HOP!**
w hop.fr

**Ryanair**
w ryanair.com

### FERRIES

**Brittany Ferries**
w brittanyferries.com

**Ferry Savers**
w ferrysavers.com

**Transmanche Ferries**
w transmanche.co.uk

### TRAINS

**Eurostar**
w eurostar.com

**Eurotunnel**
w eurotunnel.com

**SNCF**
w voyages-sncf.com

### BUS COMPANIES

**isilines**
w isilines.fr

### RIVER CRUISES

**CrosiEurope**
w croisieurope.com

**Viking River Cruises**
w vikingrivercruises.co.uk

### CYCLING

**Veloscenic cycle route**
w velocscenic.com

# Practical Information

## Passports and Visas

No visa is required for citizens of EU countries, the USA, Canada, Australia or New Zealand for stays of less than 3 months, although your passport will need to be valid for at least 3 months beyond the end of your stay. Citizens of other countries should consult their nearest French embassy or consulate for information before travelling.

## Customs

For EU citizens there are no limits on goods that can be taken into or out of France, provided they are for your personal use. Outside the EU, you may import the following allowances duty-free: 200 cigarettes or equivalent in tobacco; 1 litre of spirits (more than 22% alcohol; 2 litres if less than 22%), 4 litres of wine and 16 litres of beer; €430 (if you're travelling by air) worth of other items, eg perfume.

## Travel Safety Advice

Visitors can get up-to-date travel safety information from the UK Foreign and Commonwealth Office, the US Department of State, or Australia's Department of Foreign Affairs and Trade.

## Health Insurance

French medical treatment is very good but it can be expensive, so be sure to have good health insurance. Visitors from EU countries should be equipped with a European Health Insurance card (EHIC), which entitles them to a 70 per cent refund of the cost of any medical treatment, provided the doctor is government-registered. All other nationalities should take out private insurance. Any medical treatment, doctor's consultation and so on, has to be paid for upfront.

## Emergencies and Hospitals

In a medical emergency, contact the 24-hour **Service d'Aide Médicale Urgence (SAMU)**, which can send a doctor, an ambulance, or paramedics in a mobile intensive care unit, as appropriate. If you have an accident or fall ill in the night, go to any public hospital's *service des urgences* (accident and emergency department).

## Doctors

If you are staying in a hotel, staff should be able to recommend an English-speaking doctor, or put you in touch with the 24-hour *médecin de garde* (doctor service) that operates in every major town. If not, consult the local pharmacist or the telephone operator.

## Dentists

Dentists are listed in local *Pages Jaunes* (Yellow Pages). In an emergency, you will be seen in the accident and emergency department of a major hospital.

## Pharmacies

*Pharmacies* (chemists) – indicated by a green cross – are usually very helpful for minor ailments and injuries. Normal opening hours are 9am–7pm Monday to Saturday, but one pharmacy in every town will be open at night and at weekends; others will post the address of the out-of-hours pharmacy on their doors.

## Personal Security

Generally speaking, Normandy is a pretty safe place to travel; violent crimes are quite rare. Most crime involves petty theft, particularly from cars. Pickpockets and bag-snatchers tend to operate in city centres, usually in crowded places such as stations, trains, bars and clubs. If you are unlucky enough to have anything stolen, report it to the nearest police station straight away, and ask for a copy of the police report for your insurers.

If you lose your passport, report it to the police immediately. Next, inform your embassy or consulate – most are in Paris, though there are some consulates in Rouen, Le Havre and Caen. Make copies of all important documents and keep them separately.

Women travellers are unlikely to experience any particular problems. French men are generally courteous towards women. A firm rebuttal usually halts unwanted attention.

## Currency and Banking

France's currency is the euro. Euro banknotes come in seven denominations: 5, 10, 20, 50, 100, 200 and 500. There are eight coins: €1 and €2, and 1, 2, 5, 10, 20 and 50 cents.

You can exchange foreign currency and travellers' cheques for euros at banks, bureaux de change and American Express offices in major towns. Check exchange rates before you travel. In bureaux de change, check that the rate offered and the commission charged are reasonable. Avoid changing money in hotels as the commission rates tend to be very high. Most towns have plenty of ATMs, many of which have different language options.

Major credit and debit cards are widely accepted throughout Normandy, though some foreign cards – North American ones, in particular – may not be recognized by ATMs, unstaffed toll booths and petrol pumps. Smaller shops, hotels restaurants, and camp sites generally prefer payment in cash.

## Telephones

If calling France from overseas, use the IDD code for your country (00 or 001 in most cases), then France's country code (33), then the local number (minus the first zero). Mobile phone numbers begin with 06 and 07. Pay-as-you-go SIM cards can be bought for unlocked phones and topped up at *tabacs* (tobacconists). Roaming rates have traditionally been high, but the EU has voted to scrap high charges within member countries by mid-2017.

## Internet

Most hotels and many cafés, restaurants and bars provide free Wi-Fi access. You will usually need to ask staff for a code to access this.

## Postal Services

French post offices, easily identifiable by their yellow and blue "La Poste" sign, open 9am–noon and 2–5pm Monday to Friday, and Saturday mornings. You can buy stamps in *tabacs* (tobacconists), as well as post offices.

## TV, Radio and Newspapers

Most hotels subscribe to multilingual cable and satellite channels, which offer a variety of TV channels alongside the usual French options.

If the reception is good enough, you can listen to the radio programme *Voice of America*, which broadcasts on 90.5, 98.8 and 102.4 FM, or the BBC World Service and BBC for Europe, at 648 kHz AM.

*The International Herald Tribune*, published daily in Paris, is available on the day of publication. The pick of the local French papers are *Ouest-France* (a daily with separate departmental editions) and *Paris Normandie*.

## Opening Hours

Food shops tend to open from 9am to 7pm Monday–Saturday, with a lunch break at noon–2pm. Non-food shops generally open 9am–6pm Monday–Saturday, and also close for lunch. Hypermarkets, supermarkets, department stores and shops in city centres and tourist towns usually stay open at lunch. On Sundays most shops are closed, though some *boulangeries* and *pâtisseries* open in the morning.

Museums are generally open 10am–5pm but are closed during lunch. Most museums are closed on either Monday or Tuesday. Banks are usually open Mon–Fri 9am–4pm, with some closing over lunch.

Banks, most businesses, shops and restaurants are closed on New Year's Day, Easter Monday, 1 May (Labour Day), 8 May (VE Day), Ascension Day (40 days after Easter), Whitsun (7th Sun after Easter), Whit Monday, 14 July (Bastille Day), 15 August (Assumption), 1 November (All Saints' Day), 11 November (Armistice Day) and 25 December (Christmas Day).

## Time Difference

France is in the Central European Time Zone (GMT+1): 1 hour ahead of the UK, 6 hours ahead of Eastern Standard Time and 9 hours ahead of Pacific Standard Time.

## Electrical Appliances

Electricity runs on 220V using double, round-pin sockets. You may need to bring an adapter, and possibly a transformer (especially for US electrical appliances).

## Weather

Normandy's climate is temperate. Summers can be pleasantly hot. Spring and autumn are mild, with a fair amount of rain, but there are also wonderfully bright days. Winter is cold, but this is one of the least crowded seasons to visit and the light at this time of year can make Mont-St-Michel look almost ethereal.

## Travellers with Special Needs

France is improving facilities for visitors with special needs. All hotels, for example, are required to adapt at least one room to be wheelchair accessible, and ramps or other forms of access are gradually being added to museums and other public buildings. The Normandy tourist office website lists wheelchair-accessible sights, hotels and restaurants. **APF**, the French paraplegic organization, is also a good information source (in French only).

**Tourism for All**, in the UK, has a useful list of specialist tour operators, and **Sage Traveling** also offers a variety of packages and assistance.

## Sources of Information

The French Government Tourist Office (Atout France) has offices across the world, each with its own website holding general countrywide information. In France itself, valuable sources of information include the Normandy Tourism Board (*Comité Régional du Tourisme*), based in Évreux, while each of Normandy's five *départements* has its own **tourist office** (*Comité Départemental du Tourisme*). All have plenty of information on travel, accommodation, cultural, sporting and leisure activities, as well as special interests. It's worth consulting their websites when you are planning your trip, though the Eure site is currently available in French only.

All cities and most towns also have a state-run tourist office. Some smaller towns and villages have a private *Syndicat d'Initiative* (SI).

The **Normandie Mémoire** website has information for those wishing to visit the sites of the D-Day landings.

## Tours and Trips

A wide range of tours is available, from boat rides around the coast and leisurely cycle rides to D-Day tours.

A wonderful way to approach Mont-St-Michel is to take a guided walk across the bay at low tide. These are organized by a number of companies, including **Chemins de la Baie** and **Dans les Pas du Guide**. Guided pony treks across the bay are also available from local stables such as the **Écurie du Bec** in Genêts.

Many companies offer D-Day tours, mainly in the summer months, such as the **Caen**

**Memorial**, **Normandy Sightseeing Tours** and **Normandy Tours**, the last two based in Bayeux.

Cycling and walking tours of Normandy are offered by numerous operators, such as the US-based **Austin Adventures** and UK-based **Cycling for Softies**. **Belle France** offers a four-day "Seine Valley Secrets" self-guided walking tour, while **Classic Journeys** does a seven-day guided walking tour taking in the D-Day landing beaches and Mont-St-Michel.

Boat trips are available from many of the sea ports. One of the best is the two-hour trip from Fécamp to Étretat, which allows you to get up close to the stunning cliff formations along the Côte d'Albâtre; contact the Fécamp tourist office for details. Also fun and informative are guided river trips on the Douve and the Taute, near Carentan, which focus on the history, geography and environment of the marshlands.

There are also a range of equestrian holidays and tours. **Le Village du Cheval** in St-Michel-des-Andaines offers horse-related activities for all abilities. The Perche, with its many lanes and "voies vertes" (green paths) is ideal for horse riding, as well as for horse-and-carriage rides. The local tourist offices will have details.

## DIRECTORY

### TRAVELLERS WITH SPECIAL NEEDS

**APF**
w apf.asso.fr

**Sage Traveling**
c 1-281-547-7744
w sagetraveling.com

**Tourism for All**
c (+44) 1-539-726-111
w tourismforall.org.uk

### FRENCH TOURIST OFFICES ABROAD

**Australia**
25 Bligh St, Level 13, Sydney NSW 2000
c 02 9210 5400
w au.france.fr

**UK**
Lincoln House, 300 High Holborn, London
c 020 70 616 631
w atout-france.fr

**USA**
825 Third Ave, 29th Floor, New York, NY 10022
c 212 838 7800
w us.france.fr

### REGIONAL TOURIST BOARDS IN NORMANDY

**Calvados**
MAP D3
■ 8 rue Renoir, Caen
c 02 31 27 90 30
w calvados-tourisme.com

**Eure**
MAP H4 ■ Hôtel de Région, bd Georges Chauvin, Évreux
c 02 32 62 04 27
w eure-tourisme.fr

**Manche**
MAP C4 ■ Maison du Département, 98 rte de Candol, St-Lô
c 02 33 56 28 80
w manchetourisme.com

**Normandy**
MAP H4 ■ Le Doyenné, 14 rue Charles-Corbeau, Évreux c 02 32 33 79 00
w normandie-tourisme.fr

**Orne**
MAP E6 ■ 86 rue St-Blaise, Alençon c 02 33 28 07 00
w ornetourisme.com

**Seine-Maritime**
MAP G3 ■ 28 rue Raymond Aron, Mont Saint Aignan
c 02 35 12 10 10
w seine-maritime-tourisme.com

### TOUR AND TRIPS

**Austin Adventures**
c 800 575 1540
w austinadventures.com

**Belle France (UK)**
c 01580 849 236
w bellefrance.com

**Caen Memorial**
MAP D3 ■ Esplanade Général Eisenhower, Caen
c 02 31 06 06 45
w memorial-caen.fr

**Chemins de la Baie**
c 02 33 89 80 88
w cheminsdelabaie.com

**Classic Journeys (US)**
c 800 200 3887
w classicjourneys.com

**Cycling for Softies**
c 020 771 7760
w cycling-for-softies.co.uk

**Dans Les Pas du Guide**
c 02 33 58 44 82
w lespasduguide.com

**Écurie du Bec**
c 06 59 17 77 34
w ecuriedubec.fr

**Normandie Mémoire**
w normandiememoire.com

**Normandy Sightseeing Tours**
MAP D3 ■ 6 rue St-Jean, Bayeux
c 02 31 51 70 52
w normandy-sightseeing-tours.com

**Normandy Tours**
MAP D3 ■ 26 pl de la Gare, Bayeux
c 02 31 92 10 70
w normandy-landing-tour.com

**Le Village du Cheval**
MAP D3 w cdcdupaysdandaine.fr

## Shopping

Whether you're after some tasty cheese or a more lasting souvenir – perhaps a beautiful piece of faïence ware – you'll find plenty of good shopping possibilities.

One of the great joys of visiting Normandy is shopping in the superb weekly morning markets (marchés) that really bring country towns to life (see pp76–7). Tourist offices can supply a calendar of market days in the area. Arrive early to be sure of the best choice; most end at noon. Look out for specialist local producers with only one or two lines – perhaps cheese or cider. Their goods are often high in quality, but relatively low in price.

Apart from cider, Calvados and cheese, other local specialities include superb home-made jams, confiture de lait (a kind of milk jam), sablés d'Asnelles (a shortbread) and sucres de pomme ("apple sugars"– a type of bonbon).

If you're interested in buying local specialities, check with the tourist office to see if one of Normandy's specialist food-related markets, fairs or festivals is taking place nearby. All over Normandy, you will see roadside signs advertising vente directe (direct selling) and dégustation (tasting) of home-made produce – commonly cheese, cider and Calvados. Usually prices are much lower than in the shops.

You'll find many antiques and bric-a-brac shops in picturesque towns. Arts and crafts are sold in a number of specialist shops and craft centres. Rouen is famous for its faïence (see p90). Quality linen teacloths, tablecloths and the like can be bought from the shop in the Maison du Lin in Routot (see p90). Blangy-sur-Bresle is renowned for its glass and produces beautiful perfume bottles – you can see them being made and buy samples in the **Musée de la Verrerie**.

Normandy is close to Paris, and good clothes are never far away. Caen and Rouen are noted for boutiques and department stores, such as **Printemps** and **Galeries Lafayette**.

The Channel ports, especially Dieppe, Le Havre and Cherbourg, are popular destinations for day-trippers, mostly intent on buying alcohol in hypermarkets such as **Auchen** and **Carrefour** near the ferry terminals. The website **Day-Tripper** has details of the best deals and offers, but check the websites of ferry companies, too (see p121).

Non-EU residents can claim back the value added tax (TVA) on purchases worth more than €175 in one shop, as long as they are exported within three months.

## Where to Eat

Normandy has many superb restaurants, using fresh local ingredients. On the coast, freshly caught fish and shellfish dominate, while inland famous regional dishes, such as teurgoule and poulet Vallée d'Auge (see p72), hold sway. In towns you'll also find brasseries, similar to cafés, serving meals at most hours of the day. Restaurants are usually open noon–2pm and 7–9:30pm.

Most restaurants have several menu prix-fixe (set menus), as well as à la carte, from which you order separate dishes. By law, menus must be displayed outside the restaurant. Set menus, which may include wine, are usually excellent value, the cheapest often costing as little as €13.

There's not much to choose between places calling themselves cafés and those which call themselves bars. All serve alcoholic drinks and coffee all day, and most serve simple snacks such as ham or cheese sandwiches.

In cafés, the bill is brought to your table with your order, but there is no need to pay until you leave. In restaurants, menu prices normally include service charge; an extra 5 to 10 per cent gratuity for good service is optional.

Normandy is too fertile for the grape, which means that any wine you drink will be from another region of France. Cider and poiré (pear cider) are often preferred to accompany the rich and creamy regional cuisine. Most cider is sold in a cidre bouché (corked bottle).

Water is always drunk with meals. Even in upmarket restaurants it's acceptable to ask for a carafe d'eau (jug of tap water) rather than a bottle of mineral water.

Like all French people, the Normans love a picnic. Boulangeries (bakeries) and pâtisseries (pastry shops) offer a wonderful selection of loaves, pastries, and sweet and savoury tarts. Markets are another good source, with artisan food producers selling farm-made cheeses, patés, terrines, quiches, *tartes aux pommes*, *teurgoules*, as well as locally produced cider.

Vegetarians are poorly served in the region. Few places offer anything more than salad, omelette or cheese – soups almost always contain meat stock. However, vegetarians catering for themselves will find mouth-watering fresh fruit and vegetables, delicious cheeses and a wide variety of other dairy products.

## Where to Stay

Normandy offers a wide variety of accommodation, from simple family-run hotels to grand châteaux. Hotels can be surprisingly good value, with double rooms available from around €50 a night. If you prefer a less impersonal set-up than a hotel, **fermes auberges** (farm stays) – working farms with simple restaurants and a few bedrooms – and B&Bs (*chambres d'hôtes*) are a good option and often less expensive than hotels. Self-catering holiday homes and camping are ideal for families staying for a week or more.

Chains such as **Formule 1**, **Ibis Budget** and **Campanile**, offering clean, comfortable rooms at budget prices, cluster at motorway junctions and airports, and on the outskirts of cities. Though lacking in character, they are great for cheap stays.

More characterful are hotels belonging to the **Logis de France**, an association of over 2,800 independent hotels, promoted together for their consistently good food and reasonably priced rooms. The hotels in the **Relais et Châteaux** group are independently owned, but expected to measure up to high standards of food, service and accommodation. The buildings in which they are located are of historic importance.

Accommodation in *gîtes (see pp132–4)* is plentiful. Often these are pretty cottages or farmhouses – most of them privately owned. Crockery and kitchen utensils are supplied, and bed linen and cleaning can usually be provided for a small extra charge.

An excellent choice of holiday apartments can be found in resort areas, particularly along the Côte Fleurie.

Camp sites *(see p133)* range from small establishments in unspoiled countryside to large, well-equipped sites close to towns. Independent camping is discouraged, as is sleeping on beaches.

If you plan on visiting Normandy in high season, whether you want to stay in a grand hotel or on a camp site, it would be wise to book well ahead. Normandy is a popular destination from spring to autumn, but from early July to late August the resorts in particular are at their busiest. This is especially true of Deauville during its

August season. Some smaller hotels in rural areas close from November to March.

Book accommodation directly by phone or via the web. Sometimes a deposit may be required; in large hotels and camp sites, you can usually pay by credit or debit card. Another option is to go through an online booking website such as www.booking.com.

# Places to Stay

**PRICE CATEGORIES**

For a standard double room per night (with breakfast if included), including taxes and extra charges.

€ under €100 €€ €100–€250 €€€ over €250

## Luxury Hotels

### Belle-Isle-sur-Risle
MAP F3 ▪ 112 rte de Rouen, Pont Audemer ▪ 02 32 56 96 22 ▪ www.bellile.com ▪ €€
This idyllic 19th-century manor is set on its own little wooded island in the middle of the Risle. The 24 rooms are elegant and comfortable, while the excellent gourmet restaurant serves creative dishes using seasonal ingredients. Facilities include indoor and outdoor swimming pools.

### Grand Hôtel, Cabourg
MAP E3 ▪ Prom Marcel-Proust ▪ 02 31 91 01 79 ▪ www.mgallery.com ▪ €€
Celebrated for its association with Marcel Proust, who spent his childhood holidays here and famously described the dining room as an aquarium, this huge white edifice is still redolent of its *belle époque* heyday, with vast rooms. The façade of the hotel faces the town, while the rear opens out onto the beach.

### Hôtel Bourgtheroulde, Rouen
MAP L5 ▪ 15 pl de la Pucelle ▪ 02 35 14 50 50 ▪ www.hotelsparouen.com ▪ €€
This boutique hotel, set in a beautiful 16th-century building, has a chic atrium bar, plus a restaurant, spa and an illuminated swimming pool.

### Le Manoir des Impressionistes, Honfleur
MAP F3 ▪ 23 rte de Trouville ▪ 02 31 81 63 00 ▪ www.manoirdesimpressionnistes.com ▪ €€
Minutes away from the bustle of Honfleur, most of the rooms in this small manor overlook the Seine estuary. Each room has been styled individually, and residents have first call on the restaurant.

### Château de la Chenevière, Port-en-Bessin
MAP C3 ▪ Escures-Commes ▪ 02 31 51 25 25 ▪ www.lacheneviere.com ▪ €€€
With 19 rooms and 10 suites, this elegant 18th-century château, standing in its own parkland, has the feel of a great English country house. It makes an ideal base for visiting the D-Day beaches.

### La Ferme St-Siméon, Honfleur
MAP F3 ▪ Rue A-Marais ▪ 02 31 81 78 00 ▪ www.fermesaintsimeon.fr ▪ €€€
This ancient farmhouse on the Seine estuary, once a meeting place for Impressionist painters, is now the most luxurious (and expensive) country hotel in Normandy.

### Normandy Barrière, Deauville
MAP E3 ▪ 38 rue Mermoz ▪ 02 31 98 66 22 ▪ www.hotelsbarriere.com ▪ €€€
With its rambling timber-framed façade, this hotel has the air of a quaint Norman cottage built for a giant. Inside, there are chandeliers and columns, an indoor swimming pool around which breakfast can be served, and a handy underground passage leading to Deauville Casino, which is owned by the same hotel and leisure group.

## Hotels with Character

### Le Logis d'Eawy, St-Saëns
MAP H2 ▪ 1 rue du 31 Août ▪ 06 19 15 52 04 ▪ www.logisdeawy.com ▪ €
Enjoy a relaxing stay at this half-timbered hotel full of charming, distinctive features. With warm, friendly hosts, it is a real home from home, and makes the ideal base from which to explore the Forêt d'Eawy (see p62) and the Pays de Bray (see p61).

### Tribunal, Mortagne-au-Perche
MAP F6 ▪ 4 pl du Palais ▪ 02 33 25 04 77 ▪ www.hotel-tribunal.fr ▪ €
Occupying a handsome building with origins in the 13th century, this welcoming central hotel is an excellent base for exploring the Perche. It also has an excellent restaurant (see p117).

### Château de Goville, Le Breuil-en-Bessin

MAP C3 ■ La Coliberderie ■ 02 31 22 19 28 ■ www.chateaugoville-normandie.com ■ €€

Set in rolling countryside, this elegantly furnished 18th-century château has 12 pretty bedrooms overlooking an impeccable *jardin à la française* (French formal garden).

### Ferme de la Rançonnière, Crépon

MAP D3 ■ Rte d'Arromanches ■ 02 31 22 21 73 ■ www.ranconniere.fr ■ €€

Early inhabitants of this medieval fortified farm tried to keep people out; the present incumbents are far more welcoming. On Sundays, the two dining rooms only just manage to keep pace with the regulars. The rooms are comfortable and elegant.

### Hôtel d'Outre-Mer, Villers-sur-Mer

MAP E3 ■ 1 rue du Maréchal Leclerc ■ 02 31 87 04 64 ■ www.hotel outremer.com ■ €€

At this novel boutique-style hotel near the beach, every room is decorated in a different colour scheme. The hotel also has a quirky library with board games, and the general feel is hip but laid back.

### Le Moulin de Connelles, Connelles

MAP H3 ■ Rte d'Amfreville-sous-les-Monts ■ 02 32 59 53 33 ■ www.moulin-de-connelles.fr ■ €€

When you see the turreted mill's reflection between the lily pads that float beneath the restaurant window, you know you are in picture-postcard territory. A small, very comfortable hotel, with beautiful bathrooms and a superb restaurant.

### Perché dans le Perche, Bellou-Le-Trichard

MAP H6 ■ La Renardière ■ 02 33 25 57 96 ■ www. perchedansleperche.com ■ €€

Arguably Normandy's most unusual place to stay, this is the treehouse of your childhood dreams, kitted out with comfy beds and modern facilities, set in a 200-year-old sweet chestnut tree. The terrace completely envelops the trunk, giving panoramic views of the countryside.

## Seaside Hotels

### L'Augeval, Deauville

MAP E3 ■ 15 av Hocquart de Turtot ■ 02 31 81 13 18 ■ www.augeval.com ■ €€

In the heart of Deauville, a short distance from the casino and glitzy seafront boardwalk, the delightful L'Augeval comprises two listed Anglo-Norman-style villas. Rooms have spa baths and there is a large heated pool.

### Dormy House, Étretat

MAP F2 ■ Rte Le Havre ■ 02 35 27 07 88 ■ www. dormy-house.com ■ €€

With an Art Deco-style main building and two (rather more comfortable) annexes, this hotel sits among greenery, with fine views over the town, the sea and Étretat's famous cliffs, Falaises d'Aval and d'Amont. The breakfasts are exceptional.

### Le Flaubert, Trouville-sur-Mer

MAP E3 ■ Rue Gustave Flaubert ■ 02 31 88 37 23 ■ www.flaubert.fr ■ €€

Situated on the beach, the Flaubert is a glorious place to stay in Trouville, one of the birthplaces of Impressionism.

### Hôtel de la Marine, Barneville-Carteret

MAP A3 ■ 11 rue de Paris ■ 02 33 53 83 31 ■ www.hotelmarine.com ■ Closed mid-Dec–mid-Feb ■ €€

La Marine is well known for its Michelin-starred restaurant, which has splendid views over the harbour. But being so close to all the superb beaches on the Cotentin Peninsula's west coast, it also makes an excellent base for a seaside holiday.

### Hôtel des Ormes, Barneville-Carteret

MAP A3 ■ Prom Barbey-d'Aurevilly ■ 02 33 52 23 50 ■ www.hotel-restaurant-les-ormes.fr ■ €€

The ultimate seaside hotel in Normandy, this charming establishment sits right on the beach. It has a fine restaurant, a tranquil garden and lovely views over the marina.

### Le Landemer, Urville-Nacqueville

MAP A2 ■ 2 rue des Douanes ■ 02 33 04 05 10 ■ www.le-landemer.com ■ €€

This beautifully renovated hotel, with a fantastic restaurant, has 10 spotless rooms, each with a panoramic sea view, and some with their own private terrace. The staff are extremely helpful.

### La Terrasse, Varengeville-sur-Mer

MAP G1 ▪ Vasterival ▪ 02 35 85 12 54 ▪ www. hotel-restaurant-la-terrasse.com ▪ Closed mid-Nov–mid-Mar ▪ €€

A narrow lane winds through typical Norman countryside to the cliff's edge and this characterful small hotel with cosy rooms. There are magical sea views from the covered terrace, where meals are served in summer.

## Country Hotels

### Le Gué du Holme, St-Quentin-sur-le-Homme

MAP B5 ▪ 14 rue des Estuaires ▪ 02 33 60 63 76 ▪ www.le-gue-du-holme. com ▪ €

The chef at this hotel-restaurant – Michel Leroux – is probably the best for miles in any direction. Any thought of driving onward after your meal should be dispelled by the comfy rooms – most of them in a modern wing overlooking a rose garden.

### Verte Campagne, Trelly

MAP B4 ▪ Le Hameau Chevalier ▪ 02 33 47 65 33 ▪ www.laverte campagne.com ▪ €

This ivy-covered 16th-century Norman farmhouse retains its charming beams and bare stone walls. The bedrooms are very comfortable and the atmospheric downstairs restaurant serves thoughtful, well-presented menus of seasonal local dishes.

### Le Castel, Montpinchon

MAP B4 ▪ 02 33 17 00 45 ▪ www.le-castel-normandy.com ▪ €€

In July and August, this sumptuous château in rural surroundings specializes in all-inclusive packages for families, with accommodation in two-bedroom suites, plenty of outdoor activities for children and relaxing evening meals for the parents. For the rest of the year, it operates as a regular B&B and makes a great country retreat.

### Château de Boucéel, Vergoncey

MAP B5 ▪ Lieu-dit Boucéel ▪ 02 33 48 34 61 ▪ www.chateau debouceel.com ▪ €€

This lovely 1760s château near the Bay of Mont-St-Michel is run by the descendants of its original owners. Its palatial rooms represent superb value; there are also cottages for rent in the grounds.

### Château de la Rapée, Gisors

MAP J3 ▪ Bazincourt-sur-Epte ▪ 02 32 55 11 61 ▪ www.hotelrapee.com ▪ €€

At the end of a rutted forest track, this Gothic mansion offers spacious rooms with fine furniture, lovely views and excellent food in the restaurant.

### Le Pavillon de Gouffern, Silly-en-Gouffern

MAP E5 ▪ Rue de l'Église ▪ 02 33 36 64 26 ▪ www. pavillondegouffern.com ▪ €€

East of Argentan and close to the National Stud, this attractive

18th-century hunting lodge is set in its own wooded park, at the source of the River Orne.

### La Réserve, Giverny

MAP H4 ▪ La Réserve Fond des Marettes ▪ 02 32 21 99 09 ▪ www.giverny-lareserve.com ▪ €€

More a luxury B&B than a hotel, La Réserve is arguably the best place to stay in the Giverny area. Its five rooms are full of light and tastefully decorated with beautiful antiques and floral soft furnishings. The service is charming and personal.

### D'Une Île, Rémalard

MAP G6 ▪ Domaine de Launay, Lieu dit L'Aunay ▪ 02 33 83 01 47 ▪ www. duneile.com ▪ €€

This picturesque collection of medieval cottages in the idyllic Perche countryside contains seven beautifully renovated rooms and two family apartments. Communal dinners, made using carefully sourced local produce, are served in the converted stable block or in the delightful courtyard in warm weather.

## Chambres d'Hôte (B&B)

### Chez Nous Hôtes, Mortagne au Perche

MAP F6 ▪ 149–1515 La Genetrie, St-Hilaire-le-Chatel ▪ 02 33 83 75 79 ▪ www.cheznoushotes.fr ▪ €

Hosts Pascal and Person have created a little corner of paradise at their lovely home in the Perche, accommodating guests in three rooms, all individually decorated and full of quirky, retro furniture. There's also an outdoor heated pool and a flower-filled garden.

## Le Domaine de Pasiphae, Vimoutiers

MAP F4 ■ 13 av Foch ■ 02 33 35 97 65 ■ www. domainedepasiphae.com ■ €

Located around 10 minutes' walk from the centre of Vimoutiers and ideal for exploring the Pays d'Auge, this handsome, red-brick town house set in immaculate grounds offers three charming, rooms, one with a balcony overlooking the garden, another with its own cosy little salon. The breakfast is excellent and you can also have evening meals (barbecues in summer) with 48 hours' advance notice.

## Les Jardins d'Hélène, Giverny

MAP H4 ■ 12 rue Claude Monet ■ 02 32 21 30 68 ■ www.giverny-lesjardinsdhelene.com ■ €

Around 20 minutes' walk from Monet's garden, this attractive old house, run by a charming and welcoming hostess, has a beautiful garden and four pretty rooms, decorated in French country style. Breakfasts are excellent and include a huge range of fresh croissants and home-made jams.

## Maison du Docteur Vassaux, Saint-Saëns

MAP H2 ■ 148 rue du Docteur Vassaux ■ 02 35 61 67 28 ■ www. saintsaens-chambres-dhote.com ■ €

Henri Matisse was a frequent visitor to the Vassaux family, who once occupied this characterful, timber-framed town house in the centre of the village of Saint-Saëns, a handy overnight stop on the way to or from the port of Dieppe. The rooms are tastefully decorated and there's a lovely garden at the rear.

## Le Manoir des Lions de Tourgéville, Deauville

MAP E3 ■ Le Bourg ■ 02 31 88 84 95 ■ www. manoirlionstourgeville. com ■ €

This is a very elegant and welcoming *manoir*, with a lovely garden, just outside Deauville. The spacious rooms are decorated with lots of beautiful antiques, and equipped with modern bathrooms. Breakfasts here are sumptuous.

## Château de Sarceaux, Alençon

MAP E6 ■ Rue des Fourneaux ■ 02 33 28 85 11 ■ www.chateau-de-sarceaux.com ■ €€

Guests at this charming château, a former hunting lodge, are welcomed by the Marquis and Marquise, no less. Accommodation comprises four elegant, antique-furnished rooms, overlooking the beautiful grounds and lake, while a converted stable block can accommodate a larger group or family.

## La Cour Ste-Catherine, Honfleur

MAP F3 ■ 74 rue du Puits ■ 02 31 89 42 40 ■ www. coursaintecatherine.com ■ €€

This charming B&B, close to the old port, is housed in a 17th-century building that used to be a convent.

The five rooms (one per floor) feature en-suite bathrooms. Nearby are three self-catering apartments that sleep five.

## Jardin Gorbeau, Étretat

MAP F2 ■ 22 rue Adolphe Boissaye ■ 02 35 27 16 72 ■ www.gorbeau.com ■ €€

An elegant town house just metres from Étretat's beach, Jardin Gorbeau offers five comfortable suites. The house is surrounded by pretty gardens – full of roses, apple and pear trees – which are patrolled by three cats, and also has a spa and Jacuzzi.

## Tanquerey de la Rochaisière, Coutances

MAP B4 ■ 13 rue St-Martin ■ 06 50 57 22 55 ■ www.bandb-hotel-coutances.fr ■ €€

Right in the centre of Coutances, but located on a quiet street, this very welcoming B&B, in a 17-century town house, offers two huge and sumptuously furnished rooms. In warm weather guests can sit outside in the courtyard garden.

## Budget Hotels

### Les Agriculteurs, St-Pierre-sur-Dives

MAP E4 ■ 118 rue de Falaise ■ 02 31 20 72 78 ■ www.lesagriculteurs. com ■ €

This long-established, family-run Logis de France has a cosy atmosphere, pretty bedrooms, and a popular local restaurant serving regional food. Time your visit for the Monday market *(see p76)*.

*For a key to hotel price categories see p128*

### Le Cap, Barneville-Carteret
**MAP A3** ▪ **6 rue du Port** ▪ 02 33 53 85 89 ▪ www.hotel-le-cap.fr ▪ €
A welcoming seafront hotel, with basic but appealing rooms, some with sea views. The restaurant has a strong local following for its excellent seafood and traditional cuisine.

### La Fossardière, Omonville-la-Petite
**MAP A2** ▪ **Hameau de la Fosse** ▪ 02 33 52 19 83 ▪ www.lafossardiere.fr ▪ Closed mid-Nov–mid-Mar ▪ €
This typical old stone building, set in one of the prettiest villages on the Hague Peninsula, has been carefully restored to provide cosy lodgings. Guests are treated like royalty by the friendly hosts.

### Logis Les Ramparts, Bayeux
**MAP C3** ▪ **4 rue Bourbesneur** ▪ 02 31 92 50 40 ▪ www.lecornu.fr ▪ €
Owned by François Lecornu, the only cider producer within Bayeux town, this charming hotel has bags of character. The rooms are all non-smoking and beautifully decorated with antiques, but have no TVs. There's no disabled access.

### Moulin Fouret, Bernay
**MAP F4** ▪ **St Aubin le Vertueux** ▪ 02 32 43 19 95 ▪ www.moulin-fouret.com ▪ €
This handsome 16th-century watermill is primarily known for its high-quality restaurant,
but it also has some simple, good-value en-suite rooms, some with views of the garden or river. You can dine outside in summer in the flower-filled garden.

### La Régence, Cherbourg
**MAP B2** ▪ **42 quai de Caligny** ▪ 02 33 43 05 16 ▪ www.laregence.com ▪ €
Facing the quay, this popular bistro offers small, tastefully decorated rooms, some with spa baths. Opt for a room overlooking the port. It makes a decent base in a town that is not noted for its hotels.

### Aux 13 Arches, Portbail
**MAP A3** ▪ **9 pl Castel** ▪ 02 33 04 87 90 ▪ www.13arches.com ▪ €€
This cool little hotel-restaurant is situated right by the seashore in a tiny harbour near Barneville-Carteret. Rooms are simple and elegant and overlook a decked area.

## Self-Catering Holidays

### Allez France
www.allezfrance.com
The properties offered by this long-established UK company range from modern apartments to stone or timbered cottages, most of which are French-owned.

### Discover Normandy
www.discover-normandy.info
This company lists cottages – more than 120 of them – near a variety of attractions: among others, the D-Day landing
sites, golf courses, Mont-St-Michel and beaches. The website includes previous visitors' comments. They will also make travel arrangements for you, whether you're going by ferry, train or plane, or want to hire a car.

### French Connections
www.frenchconnections.co.uk
French Connections offers a large range of accommodation, from luxury converted barns to quaint country cottages. The majority of their houses in Normandy are owned by private individuals. The website carries full descriptions and lots of photographs of each property and, where possible, provides links to the owner's own website.

### French Country Cottages
03452 680 796 (UK) ▪ www.french-country-cottages.co.uk
The UK-based French Country Cottages offers accommodation ranging from small stone cottages to half-timbered houses, or fully modernized apartments with swimming pools.

### Gîtes de France
08 00 60 08 10 ▪ www.gites-de-france-normandie.com
The Fédération Nationale des Gîtes de France has more than 2,000 classified properties in Normandy, mostly quaint rural cottages, and should be the first stop for anyone planning a self-catering holiday in the region.

**Normandie Vacances**
01132 564 373 (UK)
■ www.normandy-holidays.co.uk
The oldest UK specialist tour operator for the region features 120 or so self-catering rural houses and cottages, some close to the sea, others in the countryside.

## Camp Sites

### Camping des Deux Rivières, Martigny
MAP H1 ■ 02 35 85 60 82 ■ www.camping-2-rivieres.com ■ Closed mid-Oct–late Mar ■ €
It's hard to believe, but this peaceful camp site tucked away on an island is only a short drive from Dieppe. There are plenty of indoor amusements, but with the Arques Forest, Varenne River and a lake on the doorstep, this is really a place for outdoor types.

### Camping de l'Ermitage, Donville-les-Bains
MAP B4 ■ 02 33 50 09 01 ■ www.camping-ermitage.com ■ Closed mid-Oct–mid-Apr ■ €
With its own delicatessen, snack bar and visiting traders, you seldom need to leave this large, well-run camp site. As well as the beach, you can ride, play tennis, or relax in the thalassotherapy centre.

### Camping de la Vée, Bagnoles-de-l'Orne
MAP D5 ■ 5 rue du Président Coty ■ 02 33 37 87 45 ■ www.campingbagnoles-delorne.com ■ Closed end Nov–Feb ■ €
The joy of La Vée is its position – close to Bagnoles (see p66) and

the Fôret des Andaines (see p63). Its 250 pitches are set in leafy surrounds, and its many amenities include a snack bar and games room.

### Camping du Vievre, St-Georges-du-Vièvre
MAP F3 ■ 02 32 42 76 79 ■ www.camping-eure-normandie.fr ■ Closed Oct–Mar ■ €
Most of the campers here are fresh-air fiends, drawn by the prospect of energetic hikes through the countryside or taxing mountain bike rides. If that sounds too much like hard work, there is also tennis, table tennis and a pool on site.

### Château le Colombier, Moyaux
MAP F3 ■ 02 31 63 63 08 ■ www.camping-lecolombier.com ■ Closed mid-Sep–Apr ■ €
A traditional, upmarket camp site – with no caravans – in the grounds of an elegant château, where (if you book) you can dine on Tuesday and Saturday. It has a heated pool, bar, crêperie, grocery, games room and mini golf. There are no karaoke nights here; instead, they stage open-air classical music recitals.

### La Côte de Nacre, St-Aubin-sur-Mer
MAP G1 ■ Rue Général Moulton ■ 02 31 97 14 45 ■ www.camping-cote-de-nacre.com ■ Closed Oct–Apr ■ €
With a superb swimming pool, water chutes, kids' activities and organized entertainment, this is a great family-oriented five-star camp site.

### Les Gravelets, Montmartin-sur-Mer
MAP B4 ■ 3 rue du Rey ■ 02 33 47 70 20 ■ Closed Nov–Mar ■ €
This two-star seaside camp site was converted from a lime quarry in 1983. One of the pits is now used for rock climbing; the other has been turned into tennis courts. You can catch your own seafood and cook it over a campfire.

### Le Ranch, Le Rozel
MAP A2 ■ 02 33 10 07 10 ■ www.camping-leranch.com ■ Closed Oct–Apr ■ €
Pitch a tent, or stay in one of the site's well-designed caravans. Situated on the west coast of the Cotentin, Le Ranch has access to a vast, fine sandy beach, a good place for serious surfing.

### La Vallée, Houlgate
MAP E3 ■ 88 rte de la Vallée ■ 02 31 24 40 69 ■ www.campinglavallee.com ■ Closed Oct–Mar ■ €
This very large and well-equipped site is just a short walk from Houlgate beach, where you can take sailing lessons and go sea fishing.

### Château de Lez Eaux, St-Pair-sur-Mer
MAP B5 ■ 02 33 51 66 09 ■ www.lez-eaux.com ■ Closed end Sep–end Mar ■ €€
Large, luxury "pitches", and wood cabins are offered at this four-star camp site. If you tire of the aquapark, tennis, volleyball and billiards, Mont-St-Michel, Granville and Brittany are all within easy reach.

*For a key to hotel price categories see p128*

# Index

# Acknowledgments

## Authors

Fiona Duncan and Leonie Glass are a British travel-writing team of long standing. They are co-authors of *DK Eyewitness Travel Guide Top 10 Amsterdam*, as well as numerous guides for Duncan Petersen, including *Paris Walks* in the *On the Foot Guide* series and several of the *Charming Small Hotel* Guides. Fiona Duncan is a frequent contributor to the *Daily Telegraph*'s Travel pages.

**Additional Contributor**
Ruth Reisenberger

**Publishing Director** Georgina Dee

**Publisher** Vivien Antwi

**Design Director** Phil Ormerod

**Editorial** Kate Berens, Michelle Crane, Rachel Fox, Scarlett O'Hara, Sally Schafer, Sophie Wright

**Design** Richard Czapnik, Bhavika Mathur, Marisa Renzullo

**Commissioned Photography** Max Alexander, Alex Havret, Rough Guides/Greg Ward, Tony Souter

**Picture Research** Susie Peachey, Ellen Root, Lucy Sienkowska, Oran Tarjan

**Cartography** Dominic Beddow, Simonetta Giori, James MacDonald, Reetu Pandey

**DTP** Jason Little, George Nimmo

**Production** Olivia Jeffries

**Factchecker** Lyn Parry

**Proofreader** Debra Wolter

**Indexer** Hilary Bird

**Illustrator** chrisorr.com

First edition created by DP Services, a division of Duncan Peterson Publishing Ltd.

**Revisions Team**
Bhavika Matur, Rada Radojicic, Aakanksha Singh.

## Picture Credits

The publisher would like to thank the following for their kind permission to reproduce their photographs:

**Key:** a-above; b-below/bottom; c-centre; f-far; l-left; r-right; t-top

**Alamy Stock Photo:** age fotostock/J.D. Dallet 55b; The Art Archive/Gianni Dagli Orti 96cla; Arterra Picture Library/Clement Philippe 21cl; David Bagnall 20bl, 21cra, 31tr; Sebastien Breham 4cl; BSIP SA/MAY 65tc; David Burton 71cl; Chronicle 50cr; EPA/Etienne Laurent 81tr;

Keith Erskine 117crb; FALKENSTEINFOTO 51cla; Wayne Farrell 77crb; Patrick Forget 94cl; garfotos 65cla; Gilles Targat 69br, 80br; Hemis 52tl, /Arnaud Chicurel 30cl, 80t, /Betrand Rieger 99cra, 111tc, /Francis Cormon 87tl, 97bl, /Franck Guiziou 32cla, 34-5, 63tr, 66cla, 72t, 78tr, 98tl, 102tl, /Hervé Hughes 7tr, 39tl, 55cr, 110cla, /Stephane Lemaire 76b, /Rene Mattes 12cb, /Philippe Renault 33crb, / Jean-Daniel Sudres 70tr, 71tr; Heritage Image Partnership Ltd *White Water Lilies* (1899)Claude Monet 49tr; imageBROKER/gourmet-vision 72clb, /White Star/Guido Schiefer 74cb; incamerastock 23br; INTERFOTO/Fine Arts 17tl; Brian Jannsen 10cra; David Jones 22cr, 23cb, 33tl; John Kellerman 25cr; Les. Ladbury 63br; Le Pictorium/Philippe Martineau 75c; Lebrecht Music and Arts Photo Library 53tr; Lessay France/Steve Frost 103cra; Photos 12/ Gilles Targat 92tl; Rolf Richardson 36cr; robertharding/Jon Miller 58-9; Richard Semik 23tl; David South 104cra; Andrew Wilson 79tr; 115tl; World Pictures 114b; Tim Wright 81cl, Robert Zehetmayer 60br.

**Bayeux-Bessin Tourisme:** Claire Beauruel 18cl; Galerie Tapisserie de Bayeux avec autorisation spéciale de la Ville de Bayeux 10cl, 16-7; Photos Calvados/Gregory Wait 18br; JM Piel 36tl.

**Galerie Tapisserie de Bayeux:** 16clb.

**Bridgeman Images:** The Barnes Foundation, Philadelphia, Pennsylvania, USA *Mussel Fishers at* Berneval (1879) by Pierre Auguste Renoir 48tl; Christie's Images *Etretat-a Windmill*; *Etretat-un moulin a Vent* by Jean Baptiste Camille Corot 48b; De Agostini Picture Library/ Bibliothèque Nationale De France, Paris *The Battle of Formigny, April 25, 1450*, miniature from The Life of Charles VII by Jean Chartier 46br; Jacques Prevert 51bl.

**Calvados Tourisme:** 64clb, 68cl, 70bl, 93cr, 95tl, 95bl.

**Corbis:** adoc-photos 47tr; AS400 DB 37b; Berliner Verlag/Archiv 47cl; Stefano Bianchetti 50tl; Massimo Borchi 88bc; Design Pics/Ian Cumming 60tl; Michael Freeman 19cl; The Gallery Collection 43b, /*On the Beach at Trouville* by Eugene Boudin 49cla; Hemis / Arnaud Chicurel 65b, /Francis Cormon 62cr, / Franck Guiziou 56t, 78b; Leemage 27cl, 46t; Frank Lukasseck 6l; Rivière/SoFood 73bl; Sygma 37r, /Sophie Bassouls 51tr; Topic Photo Agency 75bl.

**Cité de la Mer:** B.Almodovar 54bl.

**Domaine Saint Clair:** Châteaux Hôtels Collection 91tr.

**Dreamstime.com:** Valentin Armianu 4clb; Natalia Bratslavsky 4b; Briedys 13crb;

Brighton 34clb; Musat Christian 67cla, 107crb; Claudio Giovanni Colombo 26cr; Davidmartyn 103b; Delstudio 30-1; Demid 86cl; Dreamer82 109crb; Eovsyannikova 12-3; Frmolenko 24cla; Pruchasson Frederic 20ca; Lin Gang 1; Marius Godoi 32-3; Remus Grigore 98br; Jakezc 106b; Lukasz Janyst 2tl, 4t, 8-9, 31cr; Jorisvo 7cl, 15bl, 16c, 17bl; Junkgirl 14crb; Lubastock 86br; Francisco Javier Gil Oreja 11crb; Patrickwang 38-9; Peregrine 34cla, 108bl; Renaud Philippe 75tr; Philippehalle 2tr, 4cla, 20crb, 24br, 26clb, 35tl, 36bl, 38l, 44-5, 53l, 56bl, 88tr, 89cr, 97cr, 112b; Pierrot46 22cla; Ekaterina Pokrovsky 11cra; Pere Sanz 34br; Sergiyn 24-5, 85t; Jose I. Soto 14cla; Stevanzz 10br, 11tr; Topdeq 3tl, 4cr, 82-3; Tupungato 84tl; Ivonne Wierink 85cr; Xantana 67b, 100-1; Robert Zehetmayer 30br, 35br; Vladimir Zhuravlev 11tl; Zwawol 104bl.

**Fondation Claude Monet, Giverny:** 11br, 40cla, 40-1, 41tl, 43tl; Difalcone 41clb.

**Getty Images:** The Bridgeman Art Gallery/ Musee des Beaux-Arts, Orleans, France *The Entrance of Joan of Arc into Orleans on 8th May 1429* by Jean-Jacques Scherrer 27b; John Elk 10clb, 23cra; Heritage Images 19bl; Jason's Travel Photography 28-9.

**Musée des impressionnismes Giverny:** 42tl; Jean-Charles Louiset 42clb.

**Normandie Tourisme:** Nobert Coulon 108tl; Thierry Houyel 105bl; C. Lehembre 107tl.

**L'Epicier Olivier:** 90cr.

**Rex by Shutterstock:** Chriss Hellier 57cla; imageBROKER 73tr.

**Robert Harding Picture Library:** Richard Ashworth 93tr; Christian Goupi 4crb, 12bl, 13tl; Mel Longhurst 11clb, 39crb.

**SuperStock:** Hemis.fr 33c, /Bertrand Rieger 26tl.

**Tourisme Orne:** 3tr, 112cra, 113cla, 115crb, 116br, 118-9; F. Bouquerel 116tl; David Commenchal 62t; Manoir du Lys/Christian Vallee 74tl.

**Cover**

*Front and spine:* **Alamy Stock Photo:** Hemis.fr/ Francis Cormon

*Back:* **123RF.com:** Philippe Halle.

**Pull Out Map Cover**

**Alamy Stock Photo:** Hemis.fr/Francis Cormon.

All other images © Dorling Kindersley
For further information see:
www.dkimages.com

Penguin
Random
House

Printed and bound in China

First published in Great Britain in 2004 by Dorling Kindersley Limited 80 Strand, London WC2R 0RL

Copyright 2004, 2017 © Dorling Kindersley Limited

A Penguin Random House Company

17 18 19 20 10 9 8 7 6 5 4 3 2 1

**Reprinted with revisions 2006, 2008, 2010, 2012, 2014, 2017**

ISBN 978 0 2412 5690 9

MIX
Paper from
responsible sources
FSC™ C018179
www.fsc.org

# Phrase Book

## In an Emergency

| | | |
|---|---|---|
| Help! | Au secours! | oh sekoor |
| Stop! | Arrêtez! | aret-ay |
| Call… | Appelez… | apuh-lay |
| …a doctor! | …un médecin! | uñ medsañ |
| …an ambulance! | …une ambulance! | oon oñboo-loñs |
| …the police! | …la police! | lah poh-lees |
| …the fire brigade! | …les pompiers! | leh poñ-peeyay |

## Communication Essentials

| | | |
|---|---|---|
| Yes/No | Oui/Non | wee/noñ |
| Please | S'il vous plaît | seel voo play |
| Thank you | Merci | mer-see |
| Excuse me | Excusez-moi | exkoo-zay mwah |
| Hello | Bonjour | boñzhoor |
| Goodbye | Au revoir | oh ruh-vwar |
| Good night | Bonsoir | boñ-swar |
| What? | Quel, quelle? | kel, kel |
| When? | Quand? | koñ |
| Why? | Pourquoi? | poor-kwah |
| Where? | Où? | oo |

## Useful Phrases

| | | |
|---|---|---|
| How are you? | Comment allez-vous? | kom-moñ talay voo |
| Very well, Pleased to meet you. | Très bien, Enchanté de faire votre connaissance. | treh byañ oñshoñ-tay duh fehr votr kon-ay-sans |
| Where is/are…? | Où est/sont…? | oo ay/soñ |
| Which way to..? | Quelle est la direction pour..? | kel ay lah deer-ek-syoñ poor |
| Do you speak English? | Parlez-vous anglais? | par-lay voo oñg-lay |
| I don't understand. | Je ne comprends pas. | zhuh nuh kom-proñ pah |
| I'm sorry. | Excusez-moi. | exkoo-zay mwah |

## Useful Words

| | | |
|---|---|---|
| big | grand | groñ |
| small | petit | puh-tee |
| hot | chaud | show |
| cold | froid | frwah |
| good | bon | boñ |
| bad | mauvais | moh-veh |
| open | ouvert | oo-ver |
| closed | fermé | fer-meh |
| left | gauche | gohsh |
| right | droit | drwah |
| entrance | l'entrée | l'on-tray |
| exit | la sortie | sor-tee |
| toilet | les toilettes | twah-let |

## Shopping

| | | |
|---|---|---|
| How much is it? | Ça fait combien? | sa fay kom-byañ |
| What time… | A quelle heure… | ah kel urr |
| …do you open? | …êtes-vous ouvert? | et-voo oo-ver |
| …do you close? | …êtes-vous fermé? | et-voo fer-may |
| Do you have? | Est-ce que vous avez? | es-kuh voo zavay |
| I would like … | Je voudrais… | zhuh voo-dray |
| Do you take credit cards? | Est-ce que vous acceptez les cartes de crédit? | es-kuh voo zaksept-ay leh kart duh krehdee |
| This one. | Celui-ci. | suhl-wee-see |
| That one. | Celui-là. | suhl-wee-lah |
| expensive | cher | shehr |
| cheap | pas cher, bon marché, | pah shehr, boñ mar-shay |
| size, clothes | la taille | tye |
| size, shoes | la pointure | pwañ-tur |

## Types of Shop

| | | |
|---|---|---|
| antique shop | le magasin d'antiquités | maga-zañ d'oñteekee-tay |
| bakery | la boulangerie | booloñ-zhuree |
| bank | la banque | boñk |
| bookshop | la librairie | lee-brehree |
| cake shop | la pâtisserie | patee-sree |
| cheese shop | la fromagerie | fromazh-ree |
| chemist | la pharmacie | farmah-see |
| department store | le grand magasin | groñ maga-zañ |
| delicatessen | la charcuterie | sharkoot-ree |
| gift shop | le magasin de cadeaux | maga-zañ duh kadoh |
| greengrocer | le marchand de légumes | mar-shoñ duh lay-goom |
| grocery | l'alimentation | alee-moñtasyoñ |
| market | le marché | marsh-ay |
| newsagent | le magasin de journaux | maga-zañ duh zhoor-no |
| post office | la poste, le bureau de poste, le PTT | pohst, booroh duh pohst, peh-teh-teh |
| supermarket | le supermarché | soo pehr-marshay |
| tobacconist | le tabac | tabah |
| travel agent | l'agence de voyages | l'azhoñs duh vwayazh |

## Sightseeing

| | | |
|---|---|---|
| art gallery | la galerie d'art | galer-ree dart |
| bus station | la gare routière | gahr roo-tee-yehr |
| cathedral | la cathédrale | katay-dral |
| church | l'église | l'aygleez |
| garden | le jardin | zhar-dañ |
| library | la bibliothèque | beebleeo-tek |
| museum | le musée | moo-zay |
| railway station | la gare (SNCF) | gahr (es-en-say-ef) |
| tourist office | l'office du tourisme | ohfees doo tooreesm |
| town hall | l'hôtel de ville | l'ohtel duh veel |

## Staying in a Hotel

| | | |
|---|---|---|
| Do you have a vacant room? | Est-ce que vous avez une chambre? | es-kuh voo-zavay oon shambr |
| I have a reservation. | J'ai fait une réservation. | zhay fay oon rayzehrva-syoñ |
| single room | la chambre à une personne | shambr ah oon pehr-son |
| twin room | la chambre à deux lits | shambr ah duh lee |
| room with a bath, shower | la chambre avec salle de bains, une douche | shambr avek sal duh bañ, oon doosh |

| | | |
|---|---|---|
| double room, with a double bed | la chambre à deux personnes, avec un grand lit | shambr ah duh pehr-son uvek un gronñ lee |

## Eating Out

| | | |
|---|---|---|
| Have you got a table? | Avez-vous une table libre? | avay-voo oon tahbl duh leebr |
| I want to reserve a table. | Je voudrais réserver une table. | zhuh voo-dray rayzehr-vay oon tahbl |
| The bill, please. | L'addition, s'il vous plaît. | l'adee-syoñ seel voo play |
| Waitress/ waiter | Madame, Mademoiselle/ Monsieur | mah-dam, muh-demwahzel/ muh-syuh |
| menu | le menu, la carte | men-oo, kart |
| fixed-price menu | le menu à prix fixe | men-oo ah pree feeks |
| cover charge | le couvert | koo-vehr |
| wine list | la carte des vins | kart-deh vañ |
| glass | le verre | vehr |
| bottle | la bouteille | boo-tay |
| knife | le couteau | koo-toh |
| fork | la fourchette | for-shet |
| spoon | la cuillère | kwee-yehr |
| breakfast | le petit déjeuner | puh-tee deh-zhuh-nay |
| lunch | le déjeuner | deh-zhuh-nay |
| dinner | le dîner | dee-nay |
| main course | le plat principal | plah prañsee-pal |
| starter, first course | l'entrée, le hors d'oeuvre | l'oñ-tray, or-duhvr |
| dish of the day | le plat du jour | plah doo zhoor |
| wine bar | le bar à vin | bar ah vañ |
| café | le café | ka-fay |

## Menu Decoder

| | | |
|---|---|---|
| baked | cuit au four | kweet oh foor |
| beef | le boeuf | buhf |
| beer | la bière | bee-yehr |
| boiled | bouilli | boo-yee |
| bread | le pain | pan |
| butter | le beurre | burr |
| cake | le gâteau | gah-toh |
| cheese | le fromage | from-azh |
| chicken | le poulet | poo-lay |
| chips | les frites | freet |
| chocolate | le chocolat | shoko-lah |
| coffee | le café | kah-fay |
| dessert | le dessert | deh-ser |
| duck | le canard | kanar |
| egg | l'oeuf | l'uf |
| fish | le poisson | pwah-ssoñ |
| fresh fruit | le fruit frais | frwee freh |
| garlic | l'ail | l'eye |
| grilled | grillé | gree-yay |
| ham | le jambon | zhoñ-boñ |
| ice, ice cream | la glace | glas |
| lamb | l'agneau | l'anyoh |
| lemon | le citron | see-troñ |
| fresh lemon juice | le citron pressé | see-troñ presseh |
| meat | la viande | vee-yand |
| milk | le lait | leh |
| mineral water | l'eau minérale | l'oh meeney-ral |
| oil | l'huile | l'weel |

| | | |
|---|---|---|
| onions | les oignons | leh zonyoñ |
| orange juice | l'orange pressée | l'oroñzh presseh |
| pepper | le poivre | pwavr |
| pork | le porc | por |
| potatoes | les pommes de terre | pom duh tehr |
| rice | le riz | ree |
| roast | rôti | row-tee |
| salt | le sel | sel |
| sausage | la saucisse | sohsees |
| seafood | les fruits de mer | frwee duh mer |
| snails | les escargots | leh zes-kar-goh |
| soup | la soupe, le potage | soop, poh-tazh |
| steak | le bifteck, le steak | beef-tek, stek |
| sugar | le sucre | sookr |
| tea | le thé | tay |
| vegetables | les légumes | lay-goom |
| vinegar | le vinaigre | veenaygr |
| water | l'eau | l'oh |
| red wine | le vin rouge | vañ roozh |
| white wine | le vin blanc | vañ bloñ |

## Numbers

| | | |
|---|---|---|
| 0 | zéro | zeh-roh |
| 1 | un, une | uñ, oon |
| 2 | deux | duh |
| 3 | trois | trwah |
| 4 | quatre | katr |
| 5 | cinq | sañk |
| 6 | six | sees |
| 7 | sept | set |
| 8 | huit | weet |
| 9 | neuf | nerf |
| 10 | dix | dees |
| 11 | onze | oñz |
| 12 | douze | dooz |
| 13 | treize | trehz |
| 14 | quatorze | katorz |
| 15 | quinze | kañz |
| 16 | seize | sehz |
| 17 | dix-sept | dees-set |
| 18 | dix-huit | dees-weet |
| 19 | dix-neuf | dees-nerf |
| 20 | vingt | vañ |
| 30 | trente | tront |
| 40 | quarante | karoñt |
| 50 | cinquante | sañkoñt |
| 60 | soixante | swasoñt |
| 70 | soixante-dix | swasoñt-dees |
| 80 | quatre-vingts | katr-vañ |
| 90 | quatre-vingt-dix | katr-vañ-dees |
| 100 | cent | soñ |
| 1,000 | mille | meel |

## Time

| | | |
|---|---|---|
| one minute | une minute | oon mee-noot |
| one hour | une heure | oon urr |
| half an hour | une demi-heure | urr duh-me urr |
| one day | un jour | urr zhorr |
| Monday | lundi | luñ-dee |
| Tuesday | mardi | mar-dee |
| Wednesday | mercredi | mehrkruh-dee |
| Thursday | jeudi | zhuh-dee |
| Friday | vendredi | voñdruh-dee |
| Saturday | samedi | sam-dee |
| Sunday | dimanche | dee-moñsh |

# Normandy: Selected Town Index